THE
Little French Bakery
COOKBOOK

THE
Little French Bakery
COOKBOOK

SWEET & SAVORY RECIPES AND TALES FROM
A PASTRY CHEF AND HER COOKING SCHOOL

susan m. holding

Skyhorse Publishing

Skyhorse Publishing books may be purchased in bulk at special discounts for sales promotion, corporate gifts, fund-raising, or educational purposes. Special editions can also be created to specifications. For details, contact the Special Sales Department, Skyhorse Publishing, 307 West 36th Street, 11th Floor, New York, NY 10018 or info@skyhorsepublishing.com.

Skyhorse® and Skyhorse Publishing® are registered trademarks of Skyhorse Publishing, Inc.®, a Delaware corporation.

Visit our website at www.skyhorsepublishing.com.

10 9 8 7 6 5 4 3 2 1

Library of Congress Cataloging-in-Publication Data is available on file.

Cover design by Amy Lee Sullivan
Cover photo credit: Susan Holding

ISBN: 978-1-62914-551-8
Ebook ISBN: 978-1-63220-031-0

Printed in China

For Gary

CONTENTS

chapter one

LET'S GET STARTED

bonjour!

Welcome to the Little French Bakery and Cooking School. In each class at The Little French Bakery, students receive a collection of recipes based on the topic of the day. In this book, you'll find many of the recipes I've been teaching since my classes began. Some are sweet, some are savory. While some are easier than others, I've written the directions so new, aspiring cooks and bakers can be successful.

In 2010 I began blogging about pastry school experiences, baking, cooking, and life here in rural Wisconsin. My photography started out underexposed and out of focus. With the help of some great tutors, books, and classes, my photography is improving. My Canon 7D and I have become good friends. I'm delighted I was able to shoot the photos for this book. The photos of me, Gary, and our dogs were taken by Mike and Heather Krakora of Krakora Studios. Lindsey Carlyle Eastman of Lindsey Carlyle Photography took the photo of me with my camera when we were in Ireland studying food styling and photography with Beatrice Peltre, of La Tartine Gourmande.

Tucked between the recipes and photographs of this book you'll find my stories. I hope you'll be able to join me in person some day as we bake, eat, and share time together.

how did this all begin?

As a little girl, I loved to bake. My parents made a great choice when I was in kindergarten. Rather than going the Easy Bake Oven route, they gave me a set of small pans and bowls with tiny mixes for Christmas. With some adult supervision, I could make a cake and bake it in the big oven. I remember my grandma was a great cook. It was so fun standing at her side with an apron tied around me. Sometimes it was a dish towel, sometimes a pretty embroidered apron from her kitchen drawer. As I grew up, I baked in Girl Scouts for badges, baked for family events, and baked with my college roommates trying recipes in the cooking magazines and cookbooks.

Fast forward a few (ok, more than a few!) years. Like many of my students and readers, I was an enthusiastic home cook. I was working in the healthcare industry, and I was trying all kinds of recipes and enjoyed taking evening demo-style classes at local cooking stores on evenings and weekends. New pieces of cooking equipment were my favorite gifts.

One day, I decided to expand my horizons and enroll in a weekend baking class. Since my work required travel, I was accumulating many frequent flyer miles. My plan was to use some of the miles and learn more about baking. I wasn't sure where I wanted to go so I found the most recent edition of *Gourmet* magazine and looked for the ads for cooking schools. I pulled out the reader response card—you know, the little cardboard postcards that used to be tucked in between the pages. There were about one hundred numbers on the card corresponding to ads in the magazine. I circled the numbers for all the cooking schools I thought were a good match. The schools were mostly on the East or West Coast of the United States featuring weekend bread and pastry classes. My plan was right on target.

I waited for the materials to arrive. Now remember, this was pre-internet so information was gathered by phone or what is kindly referred to now as snail mail. Over the span of a few weeks, literature began to arrive: little pamphlets with schedules and class descriptions. The next step was to decide which class and when. Then came the big day. When I arrived home from work one day, there was a large, thick white envelope waiting for me. I opened the outer wrapper to find a shiny, high-quality folder containing the registration materials and information for Le Cordon Bleu, Paris. It was beautifully organized and contained all I needed to apply for culinary school. I had circled the number on the reply card by accident. I had no intention of leaving my job and heading off to school, so I set it aside and continued to review the other classes' info.

A few weeks went by. I couldn't get the Cordon Bleu folder out of my mind. What if I did go away to school? I loved school and maybe this could work. As I read all the requirements and schedules in Le Cordon Bleu's folder, I found a program they referred to as Intensive. Each part was three weeks long and held in August or December. The first class was called Pâtisserie de Base, Basic Pastry. By now the wheels were really turning. What if I took a short leave of absence from work and went to Paris to take this class? I could learn enough French to get by. I had the miles, and there must be places the school could recommend for lodging. Gary and I had a long talk about my idea. He was excited, and encouraged me take the next step.

One of the prerequisites was experience in a commercial kitchen. I found a local European-style bakery who kindly welcomed me to help with odds and ends after my real work day was finished. I got to see firsthand how a commercial kitchen works. I learned how to handle batches larger than one or two dozen, and several pieces of really big equipment. Experience, check. Now I was ready to apply.

I sent off the application and within the month was accepted into Pâtisserie de Base. Even the acceptance letter was beautiful. Each correspondence arrived *Par Avion*—Air Mail. I was going to Paris to study at Le Cordon Bleu.

After sending in my uniform sizing information, my dream was becoming a reality. I now needed to brush up on my French. And I'll be honest, it wasn't brushing up, it was essentially learning from scratch. Using tapes, CDs, books, and flashcards, I taught myself enough French to get by. Looking back, my French was terrible, but I was enthusiastic and trying my hardest.

Now that I had been accepted I needed to find a place to stay. Rather than an apartment, which seemed daunting, I looked through the hotels listed in guide books and lists provided by the school, and found a hotel in the 17th arrondissement. The description sounded lovely, was near the school, and offered a monthly rate. In my best French and with the help of notes with phonetic spelling scribbles, I called the hotel, made the reservation, and was set.

story: my first days in paris

My flight was uneventful. Upon arriving in Charles de Gaulle airport, I realized everyone really was speaking French. Nothing could have prepared me for this adventure.

My first order of business was to find a taxi. As luck would have it, a driver approached and asked if I needed a cab. How nice I thought, he's speaking English. I followed him down a stairwell and into the basement parking garage. The whole time I was thinking how odd it was that Parisian taxis didn't have any markings. He kindly placed my bags in the trunk, and off we went. About five minutes into the trip it struck me. I wasn't in a taxi, and I was clearly being kidnapped. We were on the expressway heading into central Paris going at least 60 miles per hour. Should I jump? I told him to let me out. He said, "Not here!" I realized my purse was in the trunk. How could I jump and leave my belongings in this car? He pointed to the buildings and assured me we were going to my hotel. I settled a bit when I saw buildings looking like typical postcard Paris. After what seemed like hours, we arrived at my hotel. Rather than the usual fare, he asked for much more. I paid him, thankful to be out of the fake taxi, gathered my luggage, and entered the hotel.

TIP! Don't be afraid of Paris. There is a very safe cab stand at the Paris airport. Just don't ever follow someone who approaches you asking you if you need a taxi. It's a huge scam and I was really lucky.

"Bonjour!" I said to the desk clerk. I told her my name, and she gave me a very strange look. I couldn't understand what she was saying, but I did recognize the word yesterday. What?!? I had made my reservation for the day I left home, not the day I arrived. I had forgotten to take the time change into consideration. Did I still have a room? What else could possibly go wrong? "Bien sur," she assured me. I carried my bags and my tired self to the tiny elevator and found my room.

I opened my door to find a twin bed, a desk and chair, a mini fridge, and enough room to stand at the edge of the bed and look out the window, quickly realizing things were much smaller in a French hotel room. It was 85°F outside, quite warm for Paris. My non-air–conditioned room was very warm, but the marble walls of the beautiful bathroom were so cool. I rested my cheek and forehead on it and with a huge sigh of relief, surveyed my home for the next month.

I figured out how to open the window and discovered no window screen. I stuck my head out the window to check other windows. None of the rooms had screens. Could a bird fly in? Could someone scale the building and jump in my window? I pulled the sheer curtain panel across the window so the breeze could enter, but hopefully not a bird. I rested a bit and set off on my first adventure. A Metro pass.

The Metro was just across the street. I found the booth and asked for a pass. Of course the attendant couldn't understand me, nor I her. She pointed to the pass info on the window. I needed a photo. I found a photo booth and figured out how to get the photo, took it back to her and had my first Paris document. A Carte L'Orange. A weekly renewable Metro pass. This took nearly the whole day, but I had done it. All by myself.

There was a small always-open food shop just down the street from my hotel, and a beautiful charcuterie, on the street level below the hotel. I wanted this to be "my place." I walked in, took a look at the meats and pâtés, and had to leave. My stomach just wasn't ready for the sights and smells. Jet lag was winning. I went to the little shop and found some water, cheese, bread, and crackers. I was set for a few days. Feeling miserable, I called home at least three times to tell Gary I had made a big mistake. Maybe I should come home. He reassured me, and reminded me that class would start in a few days and I'd be fine.

The next day I decided I would use my Metro pass. I know this was crazy, but I decided to go to Euro Disney. It was new, and I thought it would help pass the time and be something familiar. I got to the park, bought my ticket, and proceeded through the gates. Upon arrival at the Castle, there was a sign explaining, in French of course, how it was closed. How could the Magic Castle be closed? This was Disneyland. The sign went on to explain a special event was taking place, and the staff was sprinkling pixie dust in preparation. How could I argue with pixie dust? I walked around a bit, watched families having fun, and realized this wasn't the best idea. I took the Metro back to the hotel, had a bit more bread and cheese, and planned my next adventure, finding Le Cordon Bleu.

The next morning I went to the basement of the hotel for breakfast. Each day they set up a selection of pastries, meats, cheeses, cereals, coffee and tea. It was heavenly. I ate some baguette with cheese, drank an espresso, and studied the map. I memorized the directions so I would look confident on the street. I hopped on the Metro and stepped off at Metro stop Vaugirard, the stop nearest Le Cordon Bleu. There are at least five exits for the stop. Of course I got off and headed in exactly the wrong direction. I stopped in Shoppie, a small grocery and convenience store, and asked for directions. The clerk said, "Non." Just no. With a half smile and shrug of her shoulders. Hmm, I thought. How could she not know Le Cordon Bleu? Wasn't it a major landmark in Paris? Or at least this neighborhood? I asked a few more shopkeepers. No one knew. I sat on a bench, pulled out my map, and found my way. I set off with a better sense of direction. I turned the corner, then another, walked down the block, and in front of me at 8 rue Léon Delhomme was Le Cordon Bleu. It was unassuming, and blended into the neighborhood like all the other beautiful limestone four-story buildings in central Paris. I was ready to begin pastry school the next day.

I swear I didn't sleep a wink that night due to my nerves and excitement. The next morning, I was the first and only person in the breakfast room. After a few sips of coffee and a few bites of baguette I set off on the journey that would change my life forever. At the time, I had no idea this day would ignite a spark and passion that would lead me to the remaining classes and completion of the Diplôme de Pâtisserie over the next two years.

kitchen wisdom

Many people ask me about kitchen equipment and seek suggestions for essential tools. I'd like to share some of my favorite things to help you choose your equipment. Many are investment pieces that will last a long time.

First, your hands are your best tools: smearing dough, kneading bread, tossing and sprinkling, along with many other kitchen tasks. Wash them with hot, soapy water and use them often. Sometimes during a cooking class students are surprised when I ask them to mix certain ingredients with their fingers instead of using a utensil. It's easier and often faster to use your fingers.

Second, use a kitchen scale. Find a small scale that will switch from pounds and ounces to grams. Make sure it will weigh up to at least 5 pounds. Why a scale? Weighing ingredients will give you accuracy in baking. It won't matter if you've scooped, packed, or sprinkled the flour into the bowl. The weight will be the same. Your results will be like mine because we'll both have been using the same amounts of ingredients. In my classes, I teach both French and American style recipes. Sometimes we weigh, sometimes we measure. Weighing your pastry ingredients is a great habit. If you don't have the weight listed in the recipe, there are some great online sources and books that list the ingredient and the weight of its imperial measure. In the recipes with weights, I've added measures and vice versa. When baking, you can increase or decrease a recipe by multiplying or dividing all the ingredients in proportion. When working with large amounts of ingredients, using a scale ensures accuracy and consistent results.

UTENSILS

To accompany the scale, you'll need a few more utensils and pieces of equipment. Here are some of my favorites.

> **TIP!** If you're in Paris and looking for beautiful cookware and equipment, there are wonderful shops. Some of my favorites are E. Dehillerin, M.O.R.A, A. Simon, and G. Detou. They are located within a few blocks of each other in the Les Halles area of Paris.

- **Whisks:** One or two whisks, about 10 inches long. Not too big or narrow. I call these worker whisks. You can stir or whisk with these. You'll also find a larger balloon whisk is great for whipping cream and egg whites.

- **Spatulas:** Try different shapes and sizes. It seems you can never have too many. I like the newer silicone spatulas, which tolerate heat better. A metal offset spatula is helpful for spreading batter in pans and icing cakes. Plastic bench scrapers are great for chopping dough and scraping bowls. The straight side cuts, and curved side acts like a spatula.

- **Knives:** One paring knife, a serrated bread knife, and a chef knife you love. I really like the Santuko shape. For me it feels more secure than a traditional chefs' knife. When shopping for knives, find a knife that feels right for you. Everyone has a different feel for balance and weight. It should feel safe and comfortable in your hand. Keep them sharp.

- **Big Spoons, wooden or faux Wood:** Matfer makes great spoons that are made of the polycarbonate material, making them very sanitary, yet they feel and perform like wood. They're perfect for sauces and pâte à choux.

- **Bench scrapers, plastic or metal:** The plastic ones have a straight edge for cutting dough, and a curved edge for cleaning and gathering ingredients in a bowl.

- **Rolling Pin:** I really don't want anyone to pass up a recipe or run out and buy something they don't need. That said, a rolling pin can make or break your pastry experience. I love the rolling pins I get in Paris. They're made of boxwood, a wood known for its weightiness. I prefer no handles. Find a wine bottle, a family heirloom, or a thrift shop rolling pin. You're going to want to roll tarts, cookies, and some of the doughs as we move through the recipes.

POTS AND PANS

- **A Stock pot:** To make stock, soups, and caramelized onions, a stock pot is the perfect tool. Make sure it has a heavy bottom to prevent scorching.

- **One large and a few heavy bottomed saucepans**

- **A large skillet**

- **One great piece of Enameled Cast Iron:** A famous brand name is Le Creuset. The French company began coating cast iron cookware with porcelain enamel. The company still produces its cookware in Fresnoy-Le-Grand, France. The 5- or 6-quart covered casserole is a really nice size. You'll use this for caramelizing onions, stews, soups, mussels, and recipes requiring a nice long simmer. Once you have one, you'll have it forever.

one of the best places to shop for kitchen equipment in paris is e. dehillerin.

- **Three or Four Loaf pans:** Be sure they are good ones. No need for nonstick.

- **At least three cake pans, 2 to 3 inches tall**

- **Two half sheet pans (18x13x1 inches) with cooking racks to fit**

- **One 13x9 inch baking pan**

- **8- and 10-inch springform pans**

THE BIG STUFF: BLENDER, MIXER, KITCHEN SCALE, FOOD PROCESSOR

When I was in pastry school we made everything without the aid of electric appliances. If we needed egg whites, we whipped them. Whipped cream, we whipped it. I'm certain all the recipes in this book can be done with simple kitchen tools. Will a mixer, blender, food processor make it easier? You bet. I've tried many brands of equipment, and most do a fine job. There are a few exceptional standouts you should know about.

For the mixer, a stand mixer is great. I didn't know they existed until after college. Yes, that's really true. Up until then, I used a hand-held mixer. It did the job, but sometimes you need just a bit more power and oompf. If you decide to add a stand mixer to your *batterie de cuisine*, or collection of kitchen equipment, be sure it has enough power—325 watts is good—and a five-quart bowl is ample.

Gary and I received a food processor twenty-five years ago for a wedding present. It's still working perfectly and does a great job. I keep it close by and use it for making pestos, blending soups, and making bread crumbs, to name a few tasks. Must you use one? Maybe not, but they sure are nice. Some come with an extra little chopping bowl, which is great. Make sure the bowl is big enough for the work you're planning to do.

Until recently I had been ambivalent about blenders. They're great for making icy drinks and blending soups. Most of mine have been inexpensive and did a so-so job with ice and purees. Enter the VitaMix. After hearing rave reviews I still wasn't sure how a blender could be so great. And why is it so expensive? I'll tell you. After using one at a demo class, I was hooked. The power and perfection of the blending is great. If you're in the market for a blender and can splurge, this is the one you want.

One of my favorite kitchen tools is an immersion, or stick, blender. I plug it in right next to the stove and can quickly puree soups right in the pot. It's quick and easy. The soups aren't quite as smooth as those pureed in the blender, and sometimes it's just what I want. When you use an immersion blender, be sure to turn it off before lifting it out of the soup. Can you guess what happens?

A digital kitchen scale is very high on the list of essential tools. In the United States, home cooks typically use imperial measurement, like cups, teaspoons, and tablespoons to measure ingredients. Most of the time this works just fine. However, when you start working with bread and pastry recipes, a scale will make a difference. There are several ways to measure flour. Some scoop, some spoon and level, others pack the flour using the side of the bag. Each method will fill the measuring cup, but may fill it fuller than the recipe calls for. If you weigh your ingredients, you'll have the amount you need. Whether it's a scoop, spoon, or bowl, just weigh and it will be right every time. In France you can buy a digital scale in the section of the store with irons, hair dryers, and other small household appliances. In the United States, it's not quite that easy. Look for them in kitchen supply stores. I like the ones that go up to at least five pounds, have a tare function (to subtract the weight of your bowl), and the ability to toggle between imperial (pounds/ounces) and metric. Once you start weighing, I'm hoping you'll be hooked.

Odds & Ends

Parchment paper is important. If you're not already using parchment paper, pick up a roll at the grocery store the next time you're there. It lives in the same aisle as aluminum foil and plastic wrap. I line all my cake pans with parchment circles and my baking sheet for cookies. You'll have much more success removing your cakes from their pans. Your cookies, meringues, and sponge cake with thank you. You can also stop by kitchen supply stores and purchase big sheets. You may need to cut them in half, but the cost per sheet will be much less. You can place a sheet on your work surface when you're decorating or pounding butter. I'll be mentioning parchment paper a lot in my recipes.

A pastry bag with assorted tips is a great help. You can pipe batters and icings. I use washable bags, but a package of disposable bags works great, too. I recommend a ½-inch tip (number 10) and a large star tip to start your collection.

Kitchen string, scissors, note paper, pencils, and a ruler are all helpful tools to have nearby.

story: my first experience with a scale

It was our very first day of class. We sat quietly in the theater-style classroom, notebooks and recipe binder in hand. The chef pulled out a small flat scale and explained that we would be measuring out ingredients using a scale when we were in the kitchen. His demonstration ingredients had already been measured and placed in small cups covered in plastic wrap, each labeled with the contents and the weight. We watched and listened to the butter sablé demonstration, carefully taking notes and learning how to watch the chef and listen to the interpreter. I thought it was very important to make eye contact with the chef when I had a question versus looking at the interpreter while I asked a question. I'm not sure it made a difference to the chef, but I felt much more of a connection.

After class, we climbed the six flights of stairs with our gear and entered one of the practical kitchens. We each had an area of about 4 feet wide to work, facing another student on the other side. Below the marble countertop were refrigerators. Everything was gleaming with delicious smells wafting from the other kitchen across the hall.

We needed to gather our ingredients for the butter sablé. The recipe wasn't very difficult, and I'm pretty sure the practical was more about learning our way around the kitchen, rather than mastering a butter cookie. To complete our *mise en place*, or getting everything in its place, each student weighed and measured ingredients. First on the list: salt. If I would have thought about it, how much salt could be in a small recipe for cookies? The recipe read 5 grams. So off I went bowl and scale in hand to the salt bin. Having no exposure to metric weights, and being very overwhelmed by the whole process, I took a bowl that was about 14 inches in diameter. Not a cute little condiment bowl, a huge mixing bowl. I carefully placed the bowl on the scale, pressed the TARE button to clear the weight of the bowl, and added my 5 grams of salt. Guess how much that is? One teaspoon. I could barely find it in the bottom of the bowl. What was I thinking? I moved on to the next ingredient and quickly learned I didn't need bath basins to move ingredients around the room. After a few classes I mastered weighing and could even add one ingredient into another by pressing TARE a second time. Look for a scale and try weighing your ingredients. Soon you'll be working like a professional and have consistent results.

The Little French Bakery Cookbook

chapter two

MUST-HAVE RECIPES AND TECHNIQUES

a bit about choosing ingredients

I've collected a group of recipes, techniques, and ingredients I use a lot. They're the basis for many other recipes. They're recipes to help make other recipes great. I hope you'll enjoy them.

As you read through the recipes, you'll find a lot of butter, sugar, eggs, flour, salt, and dairy. These are the main ingredients of pastry. You'll want to use unsalted butter. Why? Because butter making is as much of an art as a science. Butter makers use salt to add flavor to their butter. The amount they add makes the butter unique from other butters. If you use unsalted butter, you don't have to guess how much salt was added, you'll add your own salt to the recipe.

Eggs come in all shapes and sizes. For my recipes, I use large-sized eggs. If you're lucky enough to have your own chickens, you can weigh the eggs to determine if you need more or less egg in your recipe. If you crack the egg into a small dish, the whole egg should weigh about 50 grams. The yolk about 20 grams, the white about 30 grams. Weighing eggs comes in handy when you've separated eggs for a recipe and would like to use the other portion in another recipe. Just multiply and weigh, and you're set.

Nearly all the recipes in this book can be made with all-purpose flour. I strongly suggest unbleached/unbromated flour. In the bread recipes, you may wish to use bread flour. While bread flour is higher in protein and will develop more gluten, the bread recipes can be made with all-purpose flour.

When selecting sugar, I use only cane sugar in my baking. In the grocery, most sugar unless marked cane sugar is beet sugar. Both should be fine, and have the same results. I've found I prefer the results of pastries and caramel made with cane sugar. For some reason, our resident summer hummingbirds prefer cane sugar, too. Based on science it shouldn't make a difference. Try both types and see if you have a preference.

Salt brings flavor to your recipes. I use fine sea salt in my recipes. You may prefer large-grain sea salt or kosher salt. Flake sea salt or *fleur de sel* is great for garnishing but isn't necessary for baking. Line up a few salts and do a tasting. You'll taste a difference between salts and may find one you prefer in your cooking.

Living in the Dairy State provides a wide selection of milk, cream, and other dairy products. I use heavy cream when called for, and 2% milk in most recipes. I find 1% or skim milk to be not quite enough butter fat, but I generally don't use whole milk. I've found that lowering the fat in the milk makes a richer chocolate flavor in cakes and hot cocoa.

NUTMEG - THAT CERTAIN JE NE SAIS QUOI

Literally, *Je ne sais quoi* means, "I don't know what." Dictionaries describe it as a pleasing, unidentifiable quality. Have you always wanted a secret ingredient? I've got one for you. Nutmeg. It's a wonderful flavor, and gives that certain *je ne sais quoi* to white sauces, soups, vegetables, pancake batter, and more. The easiest way to add nutmeg is to buy a few whole nutmegs. When you want to add the extra little something, simply grate a small bit, just a few passes with a fine grater, into your recipe. If you don't have whole nutmeg, a dash of ground nutmeg will do the trick. Ground nutmeg can lose its flavor over time, so buy small amounts and replace as necessary.

ROASTED CHERRY TOMATOES

If you're looking for an ingredient to make your savory recipes pop, just roast a pint of cherry tomatoes. Slice them in half, toss in olive oil, and roast at 350°F for 30 minutes. The juices will intensify. These are great on baguette toasts, tossed into pasta, or alone as a side dish.

TINNED PEARS, APRICOTS, AND PEACHES

I have a confession. As I've mentioned, I love presentation. Wrap something with tissue paper, add a sticker and ribbon, and I'm yours. At our first demonstration of tarts in pastry school, the chef got out the can opener and opened two cans of fruit. One contained pear halves, the other apricot halves. I thought to myself, could this be possible? Through the interpreter, he called the fruits "tinned fruits" and explained they were picked at the perfect time and poached in sugar syrup just as we would do if we have perfect pears. He also liked the texture and the consistency in the size of the fruits. Okay, this sounded good to me. It's all in the packaging. Now when I'm shopping and walking down the canned fruit aisle, I'm still not jumping for the fruit cocktail, but I've readjusted my thinking and always have some tinned fruits on hand. I can quickly make a beautiful frangipane pear tart for an impromptu dessert any time of the year.

VANILLA BEANS

There are several great brands of vanilla extract, but sometimes you really need a vanilla bean to infuse its flavor into the recipe. Vanilla beans are the seed pod of vanilla orchids. The orchids grow in regions where coffee and cacao pods also grow. This is primarily around the equator, or warm tropical regions. Three places known for vanilla production are Madagascar, Tahiti, and Mexico. The beans are similar but have slightly different flavor qualities. Madagascar beans are most commonly used in extracts and are the most available. Their flavor is the one you think of when you smell and taste vanilla—not too spicy or floral. These beans are fine for any dessert using vanilla. Tahitian beans are more floral. Typically the seeds are used in cooled desserts such as crème brûlée or

ice cream. Mexican beans are slightly more peppery or spicy. They are also good for cooled desserts where the flavor can be more pronounced.

To remove the seeds from the vanilla bean, lay the bean flat on the work surface. The vanilla bean is a tube. Using a sharp paring knife, slice the bean lengthwise, cutting through the top of the tube, not all the way through to the work surface. Carefully open the vanilla bean to expose the seeds. It will look like a thick paste. Lay the back of the paring knife horizontally against the bean. Slide the back of the knife down the bean. Press firmly, but not so hard as to scrape up the fibers inside the bean. As you slide the knife, the tiny seeds will collect on the back of the knife. The pod can be steeped and used to infuse flavor into recipes. You can also drop the beans into a small bottle of vodka or bourbon. The vanilla will infuse the liquor to create vanilla extract in about six months. About six beans in 12 ounces of liquor is a good proportion. If the beans are too tall, cut them in half and slip them into the bottle. Fill the bottle to cover the beans. I've use an old bottle from purchased vanilla extract. Just soak off and relabel your bottle. It's great to pull out an infused bean from the bottle for later use.

story: pâtisserie de base final exam

People wonder if we had any exams in pastry school. Some culinary schools have written and practical exams. We had only daily grades and practical exams. Each day we would line up our finished products on our clean workstation and present to the Chef. If we were making single pastries, we needed to find the ones that were the same size and looked the best. Even if it was only two or three, they needed to be the same. No one wants to look in a pastry case and see pastries of all different sizes, the Chef would remind us. We would stand quietly waiting for the Chef to stop with his grade book. He would poke, slice, and view the dessert from all sides with a very straight face. Then, he would give a verbal remark and record a number in his grade book. On a scale of one to five, a three would be *"pas mal,"* or not bad—but certainly not considered a good grade. It meant that some something was wrong or just didn't look right. A four on the scale was *bon*, or good. Not bad, not great, bon. What we all hoped for each day was a *"tres bien,"* very good. In the grade book there were other notes, but our only feedback was the verbal critique at the end of class.

Once each week we were graded on the Chef's observations of our organization, technique, and final product. It was a bigger grade, and the pressure was more intense. We never knew what our grades were on those days. They weren't posted, but I don't ever recall anyone failing.

At the end of the course we had our final exam. The Chef would announce a few days in advance which recipes would be used in the exam. We would enter the kitchen, draw a recipe from a hat, and prepare it for the jury of chefs to grade. After we drew the pastry name, we were given the list of ingredients and measurements. No instructions, since we were to have memorized and learned the technique from our notes and class. When time was up, or we finished, we went back to the hotel. You could assume you passed unless the school contacted you to come back and retry. The wait seemed like forever.

For our Basic Pastry exam, each student was required to prepare one pastry and an unbaked tart shell. The tart is one of the most famous and classic of French pastries. There are many, many kinds of tarts in many shapes and sizes. The tart crust is so important it was part of our final exam. We needed to prepare the tart dough and turn a perfect unbaked tart crust.

My tart crust, and Chaussons aux Pomme, the recipe I drew, turned out well, and I passed Pâtisserie de Base.

I use this crust for all of my tarts, including quiches. You can double the recipe to make two tarts. Don't try to do more than twice the recipe a time. It's much better to handle it in small batches.

Nos tarte
- Framboise
- Fraise
- Multifruit
3,

paris patisseries offer inspiration and delicious treats.

PÂTE BRISÉE (SWEET PASTRY DOUGH)

Makes one 10-inch tart crust

1¾ cups plus 2 tablespoons (200 grams) flour

7 tablespoons (100 grams) unsalted butter, cold

1⅔ tablespoons (20 grams) sugar

1 large egg

1 teaspoon (4 grams) salt

1 tablespoon water, ice cold

1. Using a knife or bench scraper, cut the butter into 1-inch pieces.

2. On your work surface, make a pile with the butter and flour. Cut the flour and butter together with a bench scraper or pastry cutter until the butter is no larger than pea sized. Work quickly so the butter does not get soft or warm.

3. Gather the butter/flour mixture and make a circle with a well in the center. It will look like a flat, wide volcano, with a 3- to 4-inch open space in the center. The chefs called this a fountain.

4. Into the center of the fountain, add the water, egg, sugar, and salt. With your fingers, swish these ingredients together until you feel that the salt and sugar are dissolved. Using the pastry/bench scraper, cut the liquid into the flour and butter. This is when you'll find out if your countertop is level! The mixture will be shaggy with streaks and bits of butter.

5. Line the dough up in a long row in front of you. The line will be about 2 inches wide, an inch high, and about 12 inches long. Using the heel of your hand, smear (about a third at a time) the dough straight ahead, taking small amounts as you work across the dough. Work left to right . . . or right to left. Once all the dough has been smeared, gather it back into the line and smear again. You'll make about two to three passes. The dough should be combined, though there will still be a few streaks of butter in the dough.

6. Flatten the dough into a disk about 6 inches in diameter and ½ inch thick. Wrap the dough in plastic wrap or parchment paper, if you plan to use the same day. Chill the dough in the refrigerator for 20 to 30 minutes.

> **TIP!** The French term for smearing the dough is *fraiser* (freh-zey). Rather than mixing the dough, it creates layers of butter and flour. When the butter heats, it melts and becomes steam, which pushes the layers of flour apart, creating a nice flaking crust. Keeping the ingredients cold and chopping rather than mixing will keep the dough light and flaky. Over-working the dough will develop the gluten, making the dough tough and elastic. Resting and chilling the dough will make it much easier to roll.

The Little French Bakery Cookbook

CHICKEN STOCK

Another go-to recipe is Chicken Stock. In a pinch there are good ones in the grocery store, but nothing beats stock made from scratch. Once I started making my own stock I never went back. Risottos and soups are so much better with homemade stock. It requires very little supervised time. Once it's finished, freeze it and you'll have stock ready in minutes. I don't use a whole chicken. Instead, I use the carcass from a roasted chicken or turkey. If I've picked up a rotisserie chicken at the market for a quick supper, I use these for stock too. The roasting adds color and and depth of flavor to the stock. Please feel free to use a whole chicken though. You'll have wonderful meat to pull off the bones and use for soups or stews.

I have two pieces of good news. You don't have to make the stock the day you need it, and you don't have to make stock the day you roast the chicken. If I don't have time to make the stock the day I make chicken, I'll pop the leftover chicken bones, skin, and meat into a freezer bag and into the freezer for another day. Sometimes, I'll save necks, wings, and backs from a cut-up chicken and add them into the stock pot.

Makes 2 to 3 quarts of stock

1–2 chicken carcasses, from roast chicken (or a whole uncooked chicken if you'd like)

Any additional wings, necks, backs

2 carrots, peeled and cut into 2-inch chunks (about 1½ cups)

2–3 stalks celery

1 large onion, quartered

10–12 whole peppercorns

Any other soup vegetables, such as leeks or turnips

2 cloves garlic

½ cup fresh parsley

3–4 stems fresh thyme

1 large piece (about 14 inches square) double-thickness cheesecloth

> **TIP!** What if you'd like to make stock, but it's winter and fresh herbs aren't growing outside your door? It's fine to use dried herbs in stock. The final straining through the cheesecloth will remove the tiny leaves. Use about 1 tablespoon dried thyme leaves and 2 tablespoons dried parsley leaves. Making stock should be relaxing and soothing. Use what you have on hand. You can even add any leftover roasted carrots and onions from your roasting pan. They'll give the stock great color and flavor. I stay away from cabbage, brussels sprouts, and peppers in my stock. To me, they add a harsh flavor I prefer not to have in the amber goodness.

1. Place the chicken parts and all other ingredients in a large stock pot. Cover with cold water. This will be about 3 to 4 quarts of water. It may only be a few quarts if your pot is smaller. Don't worry about the amount of water. Bring to a very low simmer. DO NOT STIR. As the stock begins to simmer, skim any foam off the surface. There should be tiny bubbles at the surface, but not a rolling boil or simmer. Cover the pot with the lid ajar. Simmer your stock for 3 to 6 hours. The stock should be rich and golden in color.

2. When you're ready to finish the stock, remove the stock from the heat. Line a colander with a large piece of damp cheesecloth or a clean cloth handkerchief. Place the colander over another large bowl. Without disturbing the chicken and vegetables too much, carefully ladle the stock from the pot into the colander. The bones and vegetables will stay in the colander, and the stock will filter through the cheesecloth into the bowl below. Continue until most of the liquid has been transferred. You may need to do this in batches, as well as change the cheesecloth or rinse the liner. I've heard that some people have had success using a coffee filter. I've not had that success. I prefer the cheesecloth. Quickly cool and refrigerate the stock.

3. Once the soup is chilled, the fat will rise to the surface. Using a spoon, skim the fat off the top. You'll notice we haven't salted our stock yet. I salt the final recipe, so I don't add salt to the stock. If you've used a prepared rotisserie chicken, the stock will have a bit a salt from the seasonings. To store, label with the contents and date. You can use a zip-style freezer bag, and lay it flat on the shelf. I like to divide the stock into 1-quart portions. It seems to be a perfect size for most recipes. Your stock can be stored in the refrigerator for 2 days, or frozen for up to 3 months.

TIP! I'm picky about food safety and safe handling. The best way to handle your stock is to chill it very rapidly. The best way I've found is to use a second bowl, larger than your first. Fill the bowl with ice and water. Ice and water mixed together are better at conducting cold than only ice. Set your stock bowl over the ice water. Stainless steel bowls work the best. They transfer heat and cold much better. Using an instant-read thermometer, test the temperature. When the stock is around 75–85°F, it's safe to transfer the stock into storage containers and into the refrigerator. It's best to use a container where the center of the stock is no more than 2 inches deep, or is tall and narrow. A 1-quart deli container works great.

CRÈME FRAÎCHE

Everyone should make crème fraîche at least once. It's simply magic. It won't separate when it's warm and can be whipped like cream. It's so delicious with desserts. Tangy and rich. The best of sour cream, yogurt, and whipped cream. I love presentation. To serve crème fraîche, in Paris bistros, they bring it to the table in the small enamel or ceramic pitcher with a big spoon or small ladle. Try this at home. Your guests can serve themselves by passing the pitcher around the table.

Makes about 2 cups

2 cups heavy cream
1 tablespoon buttermilk

1. In a bowl or pitcher, stir together the cream and buttermilk. Allow to stand undisturbed and uncovered at room temperature overnight, or about 8 hours. The mixture will thicken.
2. Stir gently, cover and chill until ready to use. The crème fraîche can be stored for about 10 days in refrigeration. The culture will continue to mature and will become for tangy and more sour as time progresses.
3. To serve, place a dollop on top of your pastry or tart.

chapter three

APPETIZERS AND STARTER COURSES

WARM GOAT CHEESE SALAD (SALADE DE CHÈVRE CHAUD)

One of my very favorites is this composed salad. A salade composée is served at the beginning of the French meal as an appetizer, while a simple salad with only a light dressing is served at the completion of the main course. This recipe is part of my Julia Child class, often taught in the winter.

Serves four

2 2 oz packages chèvre (soft goat cheese), well chilled or slightly frozen

3 slices stale bread, made into bread crumbs, or prepared bread crumbs

1 egg, lightly beaten

1–2 tablespoons olive oil

Salt and pepper

4–6 cups washed and dried salad greens

8 pieces thinly sliced baguette

1 batch French Vinaigrette Dressing

1. If using bread for bread crumbs, remove the crusts, and place in the food processor. Pulse the bread until fine crumbs form. Season with a few dashes of salt and pepper. Using a piece of dental floss, slice the goat cheese cross-wise into eight equal pieces, about ¾ inch thick. Place the bread crumbs on a dinner plate. Brush the goat cheese disks with beaten egg, then press into into the bread crumbs. Flip the cheese over and repeat. Preheat your oven to 350°F. Brush the baguette slices lightly with olive oil, then sprinkle with salt and pepper. Place on a baking sheet and into the oven and bake for 5 minutes, until slightly toasted.

2. Toss the greens with the dressing and divide the between four salad plates. Place two slices of toasted baguette on each plate.

3. In a skillet, swirl in and heat one to two tablespoons of olive oil over medium heat. Place the cheese disks in the hot pan. Allow to brown for 1 to 2 minutes, then carefully flip over and brown the other side. When both sides have browned, remove from the pan and place one disk on top of each baguette slice. Serve immediately.

CARAMELIZED ONION DIP

This dip is always a big hit at any party, fancy or casual. The longer you caramelize the onions, the better. I like to make the onions and the dip the same day so the flavors can marry together while the dip chills overnight. Be sure the onions are cool before proceeding with the dip. This recipe finds its way into my Entertaining and Party classes.

Makes about 2 cups

6 medium/large yellow onions

2 tablespoons butter

2 tablespoons olive oil

4 ounces cream cheese, softened

1/2 cup sour cream or Greek yogurt

1/2–2/3 cup mayonnaise (for a creamier dip, add more)

1 teaspoon salt (or to taste)

1/2 teaspoon black pepper (or to taste)

1/8–1/4 teaspoon cayenne pepper (or to taste)

1 dash of paprika for garnish

Potato chips, corn chips, vegetables, or your favorite dipper

1. Slice onions into thin strips as follows. Start by cutting off the top and bottom of the onion. Slice the onion top to bottom in half. Place the onion cut side down on the cutting board, and slice along the lines of the onion. Rotate the onion as needed to finish slicing. This technique cuts through the membranes of the onion layers and helps the onion wilt and become creamier as it caramelizes, a trick from Chef Thomas Keller. After you've cut the long strips, cut them in half again, crosswise.

2. Place a dutch oven or large pan over medium heat.

3. Add the butter and olive oil.

4. Add the onions. Reduce heat to low. When the onions are wilted, add the salt.

5. Cook over low heat for 3 to 6 hours, stirring occasionally to prevent any browning/burning. The onions will release liquid, then begin to caramelize. You may want to make a diffuser by making a long piece of aluminum foil into a ring. Set your pan on the ring to reduce the direct heat under the pan. When the onions are beginning to look slightly amber, add the remaining seasonings. Continue cooking the onions until they reach a deep caramel color.

6. Cool the onions about 15 minutes in the pan so they are at room temperature. Be sure they are not too hot. At this point the onions can be chilled and used for other recipes as well.

7. With a mixer or by hand, loosen the cream cheese. Stir in the sour cream and mayonnaise. Stir to make a smooth, creamy paste.

8. Add the onions. Stir to combine. Adjust seasonings to your taste. I like to add a little extra cayenne pepper for more heat.

9. Spoon into a serving bowl and garnish with a dash of paprika. Chill at least 1 hour.

10. Serve with chips, corn chips, crackers, or any other vegetables.

> **TIP!** For this recipe, you can substitute nonfat, low-fat, or reduced-fat products for mayo, cream cheese, or sour cream/yogurt with little change to the taste and/or texture.

SUMMER MANGO SALSA

This salsa is a favorite of our family and friends and part of my Mexican Cooking class. I've adapted this recipe from Great Good Food. Here in the Midwest, ripe mangoes can be hard to find. I use jarred refrigerated mango strips found in the produce section of the grocery store, or peaches when they're in season. The salsa is great with tortilla chips, and is also a great summer topping for grilled pork tenderloin. When I make salsa, I like all the ingredients to fit on a chip. I tend to make the dice of the ingredients smaller, about ¼ inch. It's a personal preference. Chop and dice the ingredients to your liking.

Makes about 1 quart

2 cups diced mango, or peaches

1 cup diced tomato, seeds removed

1 bell pepper (about 1 cup)

1 cup red onion, diced

1 jalapeño pepper, finely minced

3 cloves garlic, minced

1 tablespoon ground cumin

1 tablespoon oil (vegetable or olive)

4 tablespoons vinegar (red wine, apple cider, or sherry)

2 limes, zested and juiced

1 cup chopped cilantro

Hot pepper sauce (such as Tabasco), a few dashes to taste

Salt and pepper

1. In a large bowl, mix all the ingredients.

2. Cover and chill in refrigerator for at least 2 hours.

3. Serve with tortilla chips.

QUICK CHEESE CRACKERS

These crackers are great for an impromptu gathering and part of my Holiday Entertaining class. Keep the dough in the freezer, and slice off the amount you need for your guests.

Makes about 6 dozen crackers

8 ounces cheddar, coarsely grated

2 ounces Asiago or Romano, finely grated

2 ounces Parmesan, finely grated

1½ cups all-purpose flour

½ teaspoon dry mustard

½ teaspoon kosher salt

⅛–¼ teaspoon cayenne pepper

1–2 teaspoons fresh thyme, chives, rosemary, finely chopped (optional)

8 tablespoons (1 stick) unsalted butter, cut into small pieces

4 tablespoons water, plus more if needed

1. Cut the butter into the flour to make pea-sized pieces. Cut in the salt, mustard, and cheeses to blend. Make a well in the center of the dough and place the water in the center. Cut the dough into the water. Using the heel of your hand, smear the dough across the work surface to combine.

2. Gather the dough and divide into two 10-inch logs. Roll firmly so you don't have air spaces in the crackers. Wrap in wax paper or plastic wrap and chill for at least 2 hours. If you are going to freeze the dough, wrap in another layer of wrap. If the dough is soft, it will be difficult to keep the crackers round as you slice them.

3. When you are ready to bake the crackers, preheat your oven to 375°F.

4. Slice the dough into ¼-inch slices and place on a parchment-lined baking sheet. Bake for 8 to 10 minutes, or until the crackers are a light golden. Using a spatula, flip the crackers and bake for another 3 to 5 more minutes, or until the crackers are just beginning to brown on the edges. Cool and serve at room temperature. Store any baked crackers in an air-tight container.

GOAT CHEESE BUTTER AND RADISHES

Here's a spin on the classic French appetizer of butter, salt, and radishes.

1 stick unsalted butter, softened

1 small round crottin goat cheese (chèvre), room temperature

½ teaspoon fleur de sel, or to taste

1–2 bunches radishes with stems, well washed and trimmed of any wilted stems

1. Mix cheese and butter in mixer or with spoon, until smooth. Spread on small plate and top with radishes (stems and roots removed). Garnish with sea salt and enjoy!

WARM OLIVES

So simple and delicious. A spur of the moment cocktail get-together? In the Appetizer and Party classes we talk about easy, yet elegant ways to start a party. Open a jar or two of large olives. Mix any variety or color, your pick.

8–12 ounces assorted olives (avoid cheese-filled centers)

1. Preheat your oven to 300°F. Place olives in an ovenproof shallow baking dish. Bake 6 to 8 minutes until warmed through and fragrant. Serve with nuts and your favorite beverages.

SUN-DRIED TOMATO TORTA

Be sure to include this appetizer at your next party. It's a favorite. I like to teach this recipe because it's so versatile. The torta will taste best if allowed to rest overnight in the refrigerator, allowing the flavors to meld.

Serves 10 to12

½ cup prepared pesto (recipe follows if you prefer to make your own)

1 small jar (about 1 cup) sun-dried tomatoes in oil

⅓ cup tomato paste

1½ sticks unsalted butter

3 8-ounce packages cream cheese (nonfat, low fat, or regular), you will have some left over

⅓ cup grated Parmesan cheese

Salt and freshly ground black pepper

Fresh basil (garnish)

Toasted pine nuts (garnish)

Crackers or baguette slices for serving

1. In a food processor, pulse together the sun-dried tomatoes and paste until smooth. Add ⅓ cup cream cheese and process to blend. Set aside.

2. Mix the pesto with ⅓ cup cream cheese and set aside.

3. With a mixer, beat 2 cups cream cheese with the butter, season with salt and pepper. Set aside.

4. Line a small lightly oiled springform pan, or 6-cup soufflé dish with plastic wrap. Be sure to extend the wrap up and over the sides. Spread ¾ cup of the butter mixture in the bottom. Be sure to spread to the edges. Spread one half of the pesto mixture on top, a layer of the butter mixture, then the tomato mixture.

5. Continue layering in this pattern.

6. Fold the wrap over the top, and chill the torta overnight.

7. To serve, invert the torta onto your serving platter. Remove the plastic wrap and garnish with toasted pines nuts and basil leaves. Serve with crackers and thin toasted baguette slices.

Note: Keep refrigerated

For Pesto:

3–4 cloves garlic

2 cups fresh basil leaves (packed into measuring cup)

½ cup grated Parmesan cheese

¼ cup pine nuts

2–3 tablespoons olive oil

1 teaspoon lemon juice

In a food processor, pulse the garlic. Add the basil and process until minced. Add the pine nuts, cheese, and lemon juice. Process until the mixture reaches a paste-like texture. Slowly add the oil through the top with the motor running. Pulse until well blended. Season with salt and pepper.

PUFF PASTRY SALMON PUFFS

Holiday parties have been a custom at our house. They started in college with my roommates and I having people over for an end-of-semester party. We'd decorate our Christmas tree by stringing popcorn and cranberries and throwing on some tinsel. We'd always make fancy food. The tradition continued when Gary and I met. Some parties are fancier, larger, or smaller than others, but there's always a holiday party. The first year we were married, I wanted to make some really fancy appetizers—at least fancy for me. I searched through the season's magazines for delectable hot bites. Each day after work I'd prepare appetizers and squirrel them away in the freezer. The night of the party I'd bake them and serve hot, puffed treats. Some years we'd ask friends' tween-aged children to supervise the oven. They loved the job, and I loved the help. These children are grown-ups now!

These puffs are a great introduction to puff pastry and fun for holiday classes. Use store-bought pastry, or make your own. The best part is you can make them ahead and bake them directly from the freezer.

Makes about 32 puffs

2 packages frozen puff pastry

1 4-ounce tub cream cheese with salmon, or mix smoked salmon into softened cream cheese

1 cup finely chopped broccoli, uncooked (optional)

1 bunch scallions, white and light green portion, chopped

Juice of ½ lemon

½ teaspoon garlic powder

¼ teaspoon ground black pepper

1 pinch cayenne pepper (optional)

1 dash salt

1 egg, lightly beaten

1. In a medium mixing bowl, combine cream cheese, broccoli, scallions, lemon juice, and seasonings.

2. Roll the puff pastry out to ⅛–¼ inch thick. Using a small round cutter, cut the dough into 1½ to 2-inch circles. Try to cut the circles as close together as possible to use most of the pastry dough on the first pass.

3. Place ½–1 teaspoon of the salmon mixture in the center of half of the circles. Using a pastry brush or your fingertip, lightly brush the outer ¼ inch of the circle with egg. Place another piece of pastry on top, and seal by dipping a fork in water, and pressing the tines of a fork into the edge of the dough. Seal well, as the contents may ooze out during baking. Brush the top of the pastry with egg and place on a parchment-lined sheet pan. Place the pan in the freezer. When the puffs are frozen or firm to the touch, remove from the pan and place in a plastic sealable bag until ready to use. If you'd like to bake the puffs immediately, chill for 20 minutes before baking.

4. To bake: Preheat your oven to 400°F. Line a baking sheet with a silicone mat or piece of parchment paper. Place the puffs on the baking sheet (egg wash side up). Bake 12 to 15 minutes until puffed and golden brown. No matter how careful you are, some of the filling will still find a way to ooze out the sides. Don't worry, they'll still taste great! Remove to a serving platter.

SACRISTAIN (PUFF PASTRY STICKS)

These beautiful and delicious sticks will add elegance and fun to any party. They're fun to make with kids of all ages.

Makes about 24 sticks

1 sheet puff pastry (yours or store-bought)
1 egg, lightly beaten in a small bowl
2 tablespoon poppy seeds
1 tablespoon paprika
½ tablespoon garlic powder

1. Preheat your oven to 375–400°F. On a lightly floured work surface, roll the puff pastry into a rectangle approximately 12x14 inches and ⅛ inch thick. Some store-bought pastry will require slight additional rolling.

2. Brush the top of the puff pastry with the egg wash, and sprinkle with the poppy seeds. Carefully lift and flip the puff pastry over—poppy-seed side down (you may want to work on parchment paper). Brush the second side with egg wash then sprinkle with paprika and garlic powder—more or less to your taste.

3. Using a pizza cutter, cut thin strips of puff pastry, about ½ inch thick. Carefully lift the strip and twist a few times. Place the strip on a parchment-paper-lined baking sheet. Press the ends firmly against the paper to secure.

4. Repeat with the other strips. Work quickly so your puff pastry doesn't get too warm. If you feel it is getting too warm, transfer to a baking sheet and place in the freezer for 5 to 10 minutes to chill.

5. When you have all the strips twisted and secured, place in the oven and bake for 10 to 15 minutes, or until puffed and golden brown. The sacristain should remove easily from the pan. You may need to use a spatula to lift the ends off the baking sheet. Remove from the pan and serve. It's fun to present the sticks standing up in a basket, tall glasses, a vase or tied in bundles.

SPICY IN THE PAN SHRIMP

Just after we were married, we had our first big sit-down dinner party. It was late winter, and Mardi Gras seemed to be a perfect theme. Our dining room table was able to seat eight. We had invited sixteen people. I guess I wasn't thinking about coordinating the serving and seating. The menu included big pans of jambalaya and spicy pasta. This recipe was the appetizer served with lots of crusty French bread. We laughed, talked, and ate. Even our friends at the card tables had a great time. I've made these many times since for appetizer courses. Make plenty, they go fast! This midwinter class brings out the best of Mardi Gras.

Serves four to six

For the Shrimp:

2 dozen large raw shrimp (15–18 count), with shells

10 tablespoons unsalted butter, divided

3 cloves garlic, finely minced

⅓ cup beer, at room temperature

½ cup seafood or chicken stock

1 dash hot pepper sauce (optional)

For the Spice Mix:

1 teaspoon cayenne pepper

1 teaspoon ground black pepper

½ teaspoon salt

½ teaspoon crushed red pepper flakes

½ teaspoon dried thyme leaves

½ teaspoon crushed dried rosemary leaves

½ teaspoon dried oregano leaves

Crusty French bread

1. In a small bowl, mix the Spice Mix and set aside.

2. In a large skillet, melt 8 tablespoons butter (1 stick) over medium heat.

3. Add the garlic and Spice Mix. Cook for about 1 minute.

4. Add the beer, stock, and a dash of hot sauce.

5. Increase the heat to medium/high and add the shrimp. Move the pan back and forth over the heat for about 2 minutes. Moving the pan in a shaking motion helps to emulsify the butter with the other ingredients. It works much better than stirring. Be sure to be careful for hot handles and any splashes on the edge of the pan. You may need to flip the shrimp in the pan to cook on both sides.

6. Add the remaining butter; continue to move the pan in a shaking motion over the heat for another 2 minutes. The shrimp should be pink and firm. Serve in small bowls or from the pan with lots of French bread for dipping in the sauce—and napkins.

MUSSELS WITH GARLIC AND WHITE WINE

I'll admit it. I don't like raw oysters. I've tried, but just can't get past the squishy strange texture. Steamed mussels are a whole different matter. I love them. I'm not sure if it's the mussels I like, or the whole dining process. I love opening the lid of the copper pot and seeing the open, steamy mussels. There are usually friends standing by to share the fragrance. Then there's the manner of eating them. My friend Marge taught me how to eat them in a very cute way; I refer to it as the castanet method. Here's how it works. Take your first mussel and shell and remove the mussel using the fork provided. Then, using the shell from number one, pull the mussel out of shell number two. Shell number one becomes your flatware. Personally, I think it's kind of sexy. Another wonderful thing about mussels is dipping French bread into the broth. Again, proof it's not completely about the mussels themselves. I like the broth full of wine and garlic flavor as well.

Serves four

2 pounds mussels, the very freshest and best you can find

1 stick butter

4 cloves garlic, finely chopped

1 large pinch saffron

2 cups white wine

1 cup water

3 tablespoons parsley, finely minced

> **TIP!** It's very important to make sure the mussels are clean and safe to eat. Always make sure the mussels have been cleaned and the beard (strings hanging from the shell) are removed. The mussels should be tightly closed before cooking. If the shell is slightly open, tap on it, if it doesn't close, discard the mussel. I purchase our mussels at a local seafood shop. I take the package home in a cooler of ice. Be sure to ask for the best day to purchase the freshest seafood you can. After you've checked and discarded any questionable mussels, you're ready to start. Don't be disappointed if you have to discard a few before cooking and a few more after.

This will only take a few minutes. Have your guests ready, and the table ready for serving. I serve mine at the kitchen counter as an appetizer. Those guests who aren't interested in mussels will always enjoy bread, olives, and cheese.

1. In a large stock pot or dutch oven, melt the butter. Add the garlic and cook for about 1 to 2 minutes.

2. Add the wine, water, and saffron. Bring to a boil. Add the mussels to the pan all at once and quickly close the lid. Cook without opening the lid for 5 to 6 minutes. When you open the lid, the mussel shell should be wide open. Do not eat or attempt to open any unopened shells. This could also be a bad mussel. Just discard them. Serve the mussels with lots of bread.

Note: I place the pot in the center of the group with a large spoon, small plates, and soup bowls for discarding shells. Everyone serves themselves.

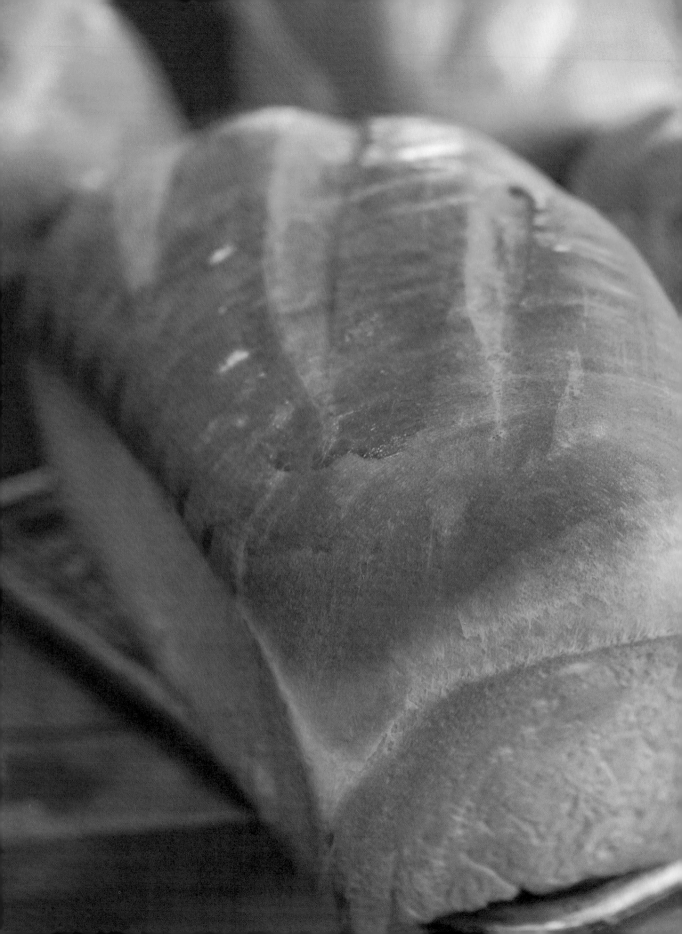

chapter four

BREADS: SPIN THREE TIMES AND FLIP

PERFECT COUNTRY SANDWICH BREAD

Classes I teach again and again are related to bread. I love working with bread dough and yeast. This bread is always part of the Bread 101 class. It's delicious and not difficult for a new bread baker. This is a wonderful loaf/pan bread perfect for toast, grilled cheese, BLTs, and best of all, French toast. The cardamom adds a beautiful fragrance and flavor.

Makes 4 hearty loaves

4 cups warm water

1⅔ cups dried milk powder

4 tablespoons melted butter, cooled slightly

1 tablespoon salt

1 cup (192 grams) granulated sugar

2 tablespoons (18 grams) active dry yeast or 2 scant tablespoons instant yeast

½ teaspoon (1–2 grams) ground cardamom

12 cups (1500 grams) all purpose flour, or bread flour

1 egg (for egg wash)

Oil or cooking spray for preparing the pans

1. If you're using active dry yeast, take ½ cup of the water and sprinkle in the yeast with 1 teaspoon sugar. Let the mixture rest until it is foamy. If using instant yeast, you're ready to go.

2. In a large bowl, combine all the ingredients except the egg.

3. Mix until it's combined and shaggy. Turn the dough out onto your work surface and cover with the bowl. Let the dough rest for 5 minutes.

4. Uncover the dough, and begin kneading. Pull the dough toward you, fold over, then pick up all the dough from the bottom and flip and slap firmly on the work surface. Repeat until the dough is smooth and you can create a gluten window.

5. Dust very lightly with flour only as necessary. Form the dough into a smooth ball, and place in a well-oiled bowl. Spin the dough three times, and then flip so the oiled side is up. Cover the bowl with plastic wrap and allow the dough to rise until doubled in size. The dough will be very tender and fragrant.

6. Gently turn the dough onto a lightly floured work surface. No punching. Divide the dough into four equal pieces. Cover with a towel, and allow the dough to rest for about 5 minutes.

7. To shape pan loaves, gently press the dough into a 6x8 inch rectangle. Try to find a part of the dough that is smooth. Place the smooth side down. Begin with one of the short sides at the top. Fold the dough down two thirds of the way. Seal with the heel of your hand. Turn the dough around so the fold is in front of you and the other short end is at the top. Fold the top toward you by two thirds and seal again. You'll have a cylinder. Place your palms on each end with thumbs on the seam and fingers bracing the back of the dough. Press with your thumbs on the seam to snug up the dough

---

TIP! What's a gluten window? To test for dough development, cut off a golf-ball–sized piece of dough. Gently stretch the dough using your fingers to help tease the dough into a thin sheet. If the dough pulls apart and tears, you need to knead a bit more. It should stretch without tearing. And, you should see light through the sheer pane of dough. If not, keep kneading. If so, you're ready for the first rise.

---

and reduce the chance of open spaces in the finished loaf. Ease the dough over onto itself, almost folding in half over the seam, and seal again. You'll now have a smooth, tube-shape of dough.

8. Place the dough in a 9x4 inch loaf pan (lightly oiled or sprayed with cooking spray), seam side down. Repeat with the three other loaves. Gently cover the pans with plastic wrap or a lightly moistened kitchen towel.

9. Allow the dough to rise until the loaves have risen 1 inch over the top of the pan. It generally takes 45 minutes to 1 hour.

10. While the dough is rising, preheat your oven to 350°F.

11. When the loaves are ready, remove the towel or wrap. Using a sharp serrated knife, or bread blade, make three diagonal slashes across the top of the bread, no deeper than ¼ inch. Whisk the egg in a small bowl, and brush of the top of the bread.

12. Place the bread in the preheated oven and bake for 25 to 30 minutes, until the bread is deep golden and the internal temperature is 180°F.

13. Remove the pans from the oven and place on a cooling rack, with bread on its side. After 1 to 2 minutes, turn the bread out of the pans and continue to cool with the bread on its side. Be sure the bread is completely baked. If the bread is underbaked, it may collapse. If so, quickly place back in the pans and bake for a few more minutes. The hardest part? Waiting 5 to 10 more minutes for the bread to finish cooling before trying a big slice. Like meat, bread needs time to finish baking even after it's out of the oven, so wait if you can.

TIP! There are many ways to check to be sure your bread is fully baked. First, insert an instant-read thermometer into the end of the loaf. The tip of the thermometer should be in the center of the loaf. The temperature should be 180°F. Second, using hot pads or oven mitts, turn a loaf out of the pan into your other hand. The sides and bottom should be a light golden brown, not pale and moist. And third, when you are holding the loaf, tap the end firmly with your index finger as if you're drumming on a desk top. You should hear a hollow sound. This is the trickiest of the tests to master. I recommend checking the temperature, and then check the other cues to learn what a finished well-baked loaf looks like.

making the french baguette

Of all the breads, baguettes are some of the trickiest to make at home. Students come from far and wide to learn the tips and tricks to get the great crust and light, airy crumb just like they've had in France. In professional ovens, steam is injected into the oven at the beginning of the baking cycle to hold the outside of the bread back while the center bakes. When the steam evaporates, the crust sets, creating a blistered, crackling crust. There are many techniques for creating crust. I think the technique I use will lead you to great bread. Oui?

Before we get started, let's talk about some of the ingredients and the role they play in bread baking.

what roles do bread ingredients play?

WATER

An essential element, water hydrates the grain. When mixed with the protein in grain, gluten is formed. Gluten is the ladder that provides places for the carbon dioxide to form, causing the bread to rise.

FLOUR

The recipes in this book are made with wheat flour or assorted grains. The higher the protein, the more gluten you can develop. Cake flour has very little protein, making it good for tender cakes, but not bread. You don't want a cake to be rubbery. Bread flour has higher protein, which makes it perfect for kneading and creating a structure for the carbon dioxide.

YEAST

Yeast metabolizes carbohydrate and produces carbon dioxide (CO_2). It's the CO_2 that makes bread rise. Yeast can be cold and even frozen, but it will die around 115–120°F. It's that temperature you'll want to keep in mind as you prepare liquid for making bread. Don't make it too warm, or you'll kill the yeast before you've even started. The warmer the environment, the more yeast produces CO_2, and vice versa. Bread will rise in a cool space; it will just take longer for the yeast to create the CO_2. When bread enters the oven, the bread has a burst of rise, which is the yeast increasing consumption of carbohydrate and expelling CO_2. Then once the dough reaches 120°F, the bread essentially stops rising as the yeast begins to die.

There are three forms of baking yeast. Cake yeast, active dry, and instant. Cake yeast looks somewhat like tofu, and can be found in the refrigerated section of the grocery. It is the mildest from of yeast.

Instant yeast is very common. The tiny grains are actually a spore surrounded by inactive yeast. Placing the yeast in water with a pinch or two of sugar will melt the capsule off the spore and wake it up to start producing CO_2. This step is referred to as "proofing the yeast." It will also demonstrate your yeast is alive and able to raise the dough. Active dry yeast is roughly 100 percent stronger than cake yeast by weight.

Instant yeast looks similar to active dry yeast, but differs in that it isn't encapsulated like active dry. Therefore, you can put instant yeast directly into recipes without proofing. Instant yeast is about 10 percent stronger than active dry. In many recipes, I use nearly the same amount and just measure a bit less if I'm using instant yeast. In groceries, bread machine yeast is the same as instant yeast. Most bread machines call for the yeast to be added but not proofed. I keep all yeast in the refrigerator. I buy it in bulk, which is more economical than the small packets.

Salt

Salt is a yeast inhibitor. While providing flavor, it also keeps the yeast in check. In some bread recipes, it's best to add the yeast and begin mixing, then add the salt. This allows the yeast time to get established.

Dairy and Fats

Eggs, milk, butter, and oil serve as dough conditioners. When added to recipes, they make the dough richer and slightly easier to work with. Since baguettes don't contain fats or diary, the dough is called "lean" dough.

French Baguette (Pain Ordinaire)

Makes 3 baguettes

Equipment

1 large mixing bowl
1 large wooden/polycarbonate mixing spoon
Measuring cups and spoons
1 baguette pan (3–4 channels)
Plastic wrap or kitchen towels

Ingredients

1 tablespoon (9 grams) active dry yeast (or scant tablespoon instant yeast)
½–1 tablespoon sugar (6–12 grams)
2–2½ cups warm water (105–110°F)
6 cups (596 grams) unbleached flour (or may use all unbleached all-purpose)
1 tablespoon salt (15 grams)
Oil/butter for coating bowl and greasing pans as needed

1. If you are using active dry yeast, sprinkle the yeast on warm water then sprinkle with sugar. Dissolve yeast and wait until foamy. If you're using instant yeast, you can skip this step and add the yeast to the flour.

2. Add the yeast/water, and all but ¼ cup of flour, together in the large bowl. Mix together with your hands or with the spoons until the dough is combined and shaggy. Turn the dough out onto your work surface, cover with the bowl, and allow the dough to rest for 5 minutes.

3. After the rest, remove the bowl from the dough and knead until gluten window is present. The dough should be moist, but no longer sticky. Clean the bowl, and then add the oil. Shape the dough into a ball. Place smooth side down into the bowl, spin three times and flip. The smooth, oiled side will be up.

4. Cover the bowl with plastic wrap and place in a comfortably warm, room temperature spot. Allow the dough to rise for at least 3 hours. Every half hour, lift one side of the dough and turn it onto the rest of the dough, and replace the wrap. Don't over handle or "punch" the dough. The movement should be gentle. This will help distribute the carbon dioxide produced by the yeast throughout the bread.

5. When your dough has completed the first rise, carefully ease it from the bowl onto your work surface.

6. Divide dough into equal portions. For the first shaping, push or press the dough with your fingers into a square about 4x4 inches. Starting at the top, fold the dough into thirds as if you are folding a letter. Turn the dough seam side down and cover. Repeat with the other portions of dough. Allow the dough to rest for 15 minutes.

7. Shape into baguettes. Using the same technique, create a rectangle 4x6 inches. Starting on the long side, fold the dough towards you about two thirds of the way and seal with the heel of your hand. Turn the dough so the top is now the bottom and repeat, folding down two thirds and

sealing. In the crease you created with the fold, place your thumbs so the tips touch and your fingers are on the top of the dough. Gently push your thumbs into the dough to "snug up" the dough. This will help prevent any open spaces in the finished baguette. Roll the top of the dough toward you one-half roll, then seal. Roll a bit more, and seal. Complete the roll and seal. Roll the small log-shaped baguette onto the seam.

8. Cover and rest for 10 minutes. Uncover the dough. Give yourself plenty of room. Using palms and fingers, roll from the center out, gently rolling the dough to the length of your pan. Lift the dough and set in the pan. When you've finished all the baguettes, cover and allow to rise for 1 to 1¼ hours.

9. While your bread is rising, preheat your oven to 450°F.

10. When the rise is complete, make 4- to 5¼-inch diagonal slashes across the top of the bread. This will help the bread expand and not burst out the sides in unexpected places. Try to start each slash just before the previous one ends. This will prevent bursts on the top.

11. Mist the loaves with water just before placing in oven. Place in 450 °F oven, then immediately reduce the oven temperature to 425°F.

12. Bake for 8 to 10 minutes, reduce oven to 375–400°F and finish baking for approximately 15 to 20 minutes more. The bread should be medium to deep golden brown. Turn off the oven, remove the bread from the pans, and place the bread back in the oven directly on the oven rack. After 5 minutes, open the oven door slightly, a few inches. Allow the baguettes to cool in the oven. This will help set the crust.

TIP! Baguettes have a short shelf life and should be eaten within 1 to 5 hours. If you need to store your bread, wrap in plastic wrap. Your bread may soften. To recrisp, place in 350 °F oven for 5 to 10 minutes. To freeze, roll in long strips of plastic wrap, twist the ends, then place in grocery bags. Try to create several layers between the bread and the freezer environment.

FRENCH FOUGASSE

This is the first bread we make in the French Bread classes. Students can't believe they've made such a delicious bread. It's a great recipe for learning to knead bread dough. There's only one rise to this recipe. If you rest the dough overnight, there will be more blistering and bubbles on the surface of the bread. If you are making the dough and baking the same day, it will be fine—just less blistering. Fougasse, meaning ladder, is a wonderful appetizer with olives, spreads, and wine. Guests can pull the bread apart, or you can precut it and place in a basket.

This is one of the breads I made and sold at a local tavern. On Thursday nights, customers would arrive as early as 4:00 pm to purchase bread. They purchased fougasse to enjoy with a cold beer and a visit with neighbors. In the beginning, it got named pretzel bread for its shape. Now, nearly everyone in the area knows the correct name and even pronounces it correctly. Tres bien!

I love the cracker-like center, others like the softer bread-stick edges.

Makes 3 fougasse

2 tablespoons active dry yeast, or 1¾ tablespoon instant yeast

2¼–2½ cups warm water (105–110°F)

6½ cups (646 grams) unbleached all-purpose flour

4 teaspoons (20 grams) salt

¼ cup olive oil

Oil/butter for coating bowl and greasing pans as needed

Olive oil for basting

Herbes de Provence, coarse salt, or your favorite dried herbs

Optional add-ins: rosemary, chopped olives, grated cheeses, or raisins

1. If you're using active dry yeast, sprinkle it over ½ cup warm water and wait until the yeast is foamy. Add the yeast to the flour, remaining water, salt, and oil.

2. Mix dough until it's shaggy, then turn the dough out onto your work surface, and cover with the mixing bowl. Let the dough rest for 5 minutes.

3. Knead the dough until smooth, elastic, and you can make a gluten window. Shape the dough into a smooth ball and place in a well-oiled mixing bowl. Spin three times and flip to turn the dough to cover lightly with oil.

4. Cover the bowl with plastic wrap and allow the dough to rise until doubled. When the dough is ready, gently turn the dough out onto your work surface. If you can rest the dough overnight, divide it into three equal pieces.

5. Place the dough into well-oiled zip-top plastic bags and into the refrigerator overnight.

6. When you're ready to bake the fougasse, remove from refrigerator at least 2 hours before baking to allow the dough to return to room temperature. If you're adding olives or cheese into the dough, knead it in now and allow the dough to rest for another 5 minutes.

7. Before you begin shaping the dough, preheat your oven to 425°F.

8. To shape the fougasse, stretch the dough into oval shape, approximately 12 x 8 inches. The oval should be slightly narrower at one end. Use the backs of your hands to gently stretch the dough. Place the dough on a parchment-lined baking sheet. With a small, sharp knife, slice two long slits vertically down the center, and three on a diagonal on each side. Gently pull the slices open to create holes in the dough. Brush the dough with olive oil. Sprinkle with herbes de Provence, and salt (if desired). Mist the dough just before placing in the oven.

9. Place the pan in the oven and bake for approximately 15 to 20 minutes or until golden brown. You may need to rotate your pans half way through the baking time.

10. Remove the pans from the oven and brush the fougasse again with more olive oil. Cool and serve.

Honey Multigrain Wheat Bread

Breads 101 introduces students to pre-fermented doughs. This recipe uses a poolish, or a slightly pre-fermented dough to start. The pre-fermentation of a portion of the dough helps hydrate the whole wheat flour, making the bread easier to knead and work with. The honey gives the bread a wonderful taste and texture. We learned in pastry school that *poolish* is derived from the French word for Polish, though *Polonais* is really the French word for Polish. Bakers from Poland were highly regarded for their baking skills by French kings. They used preferments to start their breads. The French bakers called the pre-ferment poolish, and the name continues today.

Makes 3 loaves

For the poolish:

3 cups warm water (105°F)

1 tablespoon (15 grams) active dry or instant yeast

⅓ cup honey

5 cups (497 grams) whole wheat flour

For the final dough:

To the Poolish, add:

3½ cups (approx. 348 grams) multigrain flour

3 tablespoons butter, plus extra for finishing loaves

1 tablespoon salt (15 grams)

1. In a large bowl, mix all the ingredients together, cover the bowl with a kitchen towel, and set aside for at least 30 minutes.

2. Mix dough, then knead until you can create a gluten window. It will be trickier to make the window since some of the grains have sharp edges that may tear the dough as you stretch. The dough should be smooth and tender. If in doubt, rest the dough and knead more than you think, about 7 to 10 minutes.

3. Place the dough in a well-oiled bowl, and cover with plastic wrap or a kitchen towel. Allow the dough to rise until doubled, about 1 to 1½ hours.

4. Gently turn the dough onto your work surface and divide into three equal parts. Cover with a towel, and allow the dough to rest for about 5 minutes.

5. To shape pan loaves, gently press one portion of the dough into a 6x9 inch rectangle. Try to find a part of the dough that is smooth. Place the smooth side down. Begin with one of the short sides at the top. Fold the dough down two thirds of the way. Seal with the heel of your hand. Turn the dough around so the fold is in front of you and the other short end is at the top. Fold the top toward you by two thirds and seal again. You'll have a cylinder. Place your palms on each end with thumbs on the seam and fingers bracing the back of the dough. Press with your thumbs on the seam to snug up the dough and reduce the chance of open spaces in the finished loaf. Ease the dough over onto itself, almost folding in half over the seam, and seal again. You'll now have a smooth tube of dough.

6. Place the dough in an oiled or buttered 9x4 inch loaf pan, seam side down. Repeat with the other loaves.

7. Gently cover the pans with plastic wrap or a lightly moistened kitchen towel.

8. While the bread is rising, preheat your oven to 350°F.

9. When the dough has risen about 1 inch above its pan, place in the oven and bake for 30 minutes until golden brown and the internal temperature is 180°F.

10. Place the pans on a cooling rack for 2 minutes, then turn the bread out of the pans. Brush the top of each loaf with softened butter, then cool the loaves on their sides.

a quiet sunny morning in paris should include a trip to the market

and boulangerie for fresh vegetables, cheeses, and delicious breads.

PISSALADIERE

1 recipe baguette dough, with first rise
    complete

1 recipe caramelized onions

½ cup olive oil

4 ounces goat cheese (chèvre)

6 ounces pitted Niçoise or Calamata
    olives

1–2 springs fresh rosemary

1. Preheat your oven to 375°F.

2. After the baguette dough has completed the second rise, stretch the dough on the baking sheet to
    cover the pan. The dough will be about ½ inch thick. It the dough is resisting, cover and rest for
    5 minutes. The dough will relax and be much easier to stretch.

3. Lightly brush the dough with olive oil, then spread with the caramelized onions. Place large coin-
    sized pieces of goat cheese on top of the onions, then scatter the olives on top. Coarsely chop the
    rosemary and scatter on top.

4. Place the pan in the center of the oven. Bake 20 to 25 minutes until the edges are golden and the
    toppings are bubbling.

5. Remove from the oven, and allow the pissaladiere to cool in the pan. Slide the bread out of the
    pan onto a cutting surface. Using a large knife or pizza cutter, cut the pissaladiere into 2- to 6-inch
    squares. Serve warm or at room temperature.

SPICY ROUND CHEESE BREAD

When The Little French Bakery participates in a farmers' market, this is one of our best-selling items. It continues to be a class favorite. It's so fun stretching the huge batch of dough the length of the countertop then piling on the cheddar cheese. We use a Parisian Herb blend from Penzey's Spices. Use any combination of fresh or dried herbs that appeals to you. Try different combinations, depending on what is in season and on hand.

Makes four round loaves

7 cups (696 grams) unbleached all-purpose or bread flour

1 tablespoon (15 grams) salt

4 tablespoons brown sugar

¼ cup warm water (about 105°F)

1 12-ounce bottle beer, at room temperature

1 cup milk (whole, 2 or 1 percent, or skim)

¼ cup vegetable oil or unsalted butter, at room temperature

2 tablespoons (19 grams) active dry or instant yeast (proof active yeast in ¼ cup water)

2–3 tablespoons fresh herbs, or 2–3 teaspoons dried herbs such as chives, tarragon, parsley

½–1 teaspoon red chili flakes (more or less depending on your desired spiciness)

2–3 cups (8–12 ounces) grated cheddar cheese (depending on how much cheese you like)

1 egg for egg wash

1. If you are using active dry yeast, dissolve it in ¼ cup water with a pinch of sugar. When the mixture is foamy, you're ready to proceed.

2. In a large mixing bowl, combine all the ingredients except the cheese and herbs. Mix until a shaggy, squishy dough forms. Turn the dough out on the work surface and cover with the mixing bowl for 5 minutes.

3. Sprinkle the herbs on the dough and knead to distribute through the dough. Begin kneading. Knead in the pull-fold-flip/slap method until you can form a gluten window. The dried herbs may tear the dough as you make the window, but the dough is tender and should make a window fairly easily.

4. Shape the dough into a smooth ball, and place in a well-oiled bowl. Spin three times and flip. Cover with plastic wrap, and allow to rise for about 1 hour, or until the dough has doubled in bulk. If the liquids you used were cool, it may take longer.

5. When the dough is ready, gently ease it from the bowl onto your lightly floured work surface. Stretch the dough into a 20x12 inch rectangle. Sprinkle the dough with grated cheese, keeping about 1 inch from each edge clear of cheese. Starting on the long side, roll the dough, jellyroll style. Seal the edge by pinching the seam firmly.

6. With a serrated knife, slice the log of dough into four pieces. Turn each piece and place cut side up. Each piece will be about 5 inches tall. Place on a parchment-lined baking sheet, spaced evenly. You may need to use two baking sheets. With the palm of your hand, press evenly and firmly to flatten and spread the dough. The dough should be about 1½ to 2 inches tall and about 6 to 8 inches in diameter.

7. Cover lightly with plastic wrap and allow to rise for 45 minutes to 1 hour, until the loaves are expanded and puffy. While the bread is rising, preheat your oven to 350°F.

8. Just before baking, whisk the egg with a fork, and using a pastry brush, brush the loaves with the egg wash.

9. Place the pan in your oven. Bake for approximately 25 minutes, or until the loaves are golden brown and an instant-read thermometer reads 180°F when inserted into the center of a loaf. Transfer loaves from the pan to a cooling rack and cool.

10. Slice in wedges, or crosswise for toasting. Who am I kidding? Most people tear it apart and enjoy with friends and family!

Pizza Dough Italian Style

In 2009 we built a wood-fired oven just outside the bakery building. Each time we make plans to use the oven we have every intention of making food other than pizza. Yet, it's almost always pizza. This crust is based on the Napoletana style. You can find Tipo 00 flour in Italian specialty shops and online. The high protein flour has a very fine texture, making a great dough that is easy to stretch into beautiful crusts. If you don't have a wood oven, don't worry. Stretch the dough and place on a baking sheet. Add your favorite toppings (easy on the sauces) and bake at 425°F. This class is repeated in a local cooking store at least twice a year. Here at the bakery, wood-fired classes quickly turn from class into a party!

Makes dough for four 10–12 inch pizzas

3 cups unbleached flour or Tipo 00

1 teaspoon salt

2 teaspoons instant yeast, or 2¼ teaspoons active dry (proof in water before adding with ingredients)

2 tablespoons olive oil

1 cup water (105–110°F)

1. Mix all ingredients in a bowl until combined. Let dough rest 5 minutes. Knead or mix with dough hook until dough passes the gluten window test.

2. Place in oiled bowl until doubled in size. Divide into four equal pieces.

3. Shape the pieces into smooth balls. Gently pat with olive oil to keep the surface of the dough from drying.

4. Allow dough at rest at least 30 minutes before shaping into pizzas. The dough is best when made the day before, and rested overnight. Bring to room temperature before shaping.

5. When ready for pizza, preheat your oven to 450°F.

6. Stretch the dough into a 10-inch circle. Top with sauce (sparingly) and your favorite toppings. If baking in a conventional oven, bake for 7 to 12 minutes, until bubbling and golden brown. For a wood-fired oven, heat to 800–850°F. Insert into oven and bake 90 seconds. Remove with a peel and slice.

PIZZA DOUGH ALL-AMERICAN STYLE

This dough is enriched with sugar and milk to make a richer, more tender crust. I've adapted it from one of Peter Reinhart's *American Pie* pizza dough recipes.

Makes three to four 10–12 inch pizzas

1 teaspoon instant yeast

5 cups (500 grams) unbleached flour

3 tablespoons sugar

2 teaspoons salt

¼ cup olive or vegetable oil

1 cup milk (1 or 2 percent or whole milk)

¾ cup room temperature water

1. Mix all ingredients in a bowl until combined. Turn the dough onto your work surface and cover with the mixing bowl for at least 5 minutes. When ready, knead the dough until you can create a gluten window.

2. Shape the dough into a smooth ball and place in a well-oiled bowl. Cover with plastic wrap and allow the dough to rest for 1 hour. The dough will not double, but will expand a bit.

3. If you are going to use the dough the same day, divide into four equal pieces and place on a well-oiled pan.

4. Gently pat the surfaces of the ball with oil and cover. Rest at least 20–30 minutes before shaping into pizza.

5. If you are planning to make pizza the next day, gently push the dough down, cover, and place in the refrigerator.

6. The next day remove the dough from refrigerator and place it on a lightly floured surface, covered with a damp kitchen towel or plastic wrap. I find it takes a least 2 hours to warm the dough to room temperature before using.

7. When at room temperature, shape the dough into balls, cover, and allow to rest at least 30 minutes before shaping into pizzas.

FAMILY FEAST DINNER ROLLS

Our family loves bread. All sorts of bread. When it comes to rolls, we're crazy about fluffy, soft dinner rolls. Here's a Bread 101 class recipe sure to please your family. This is a great recipe for new bakers. The enriched dough is easy to work with and produces delicious rolls.

Makes 24 rolls

1 (2½ teaspoon) packet active dry yeast or 2½ teaspoons instant yeast

1–1⅛ cups lukewarm water (100–110°F)

3 cups all-purpose flour

1 teaspoon salt

3 tablespoons sugar

6 tablespoons unsalted butter, at room temperature

¼ cup nonfat dry milk

½ cup instant mashed potato flakes (just potato, not mix)

1. If you're using active dry yeast, dissolve it with a pinch of sugar in 2 tablespoons of the lukewarm water until it shows bubbles and foam. If you're using instant yeast, you don't need this step.

2. Combine the dissolved yeast (or instant yeast) with the remainder of the ingredients.

3. Mix with your hands, wooden spoon, or dough hook on a stand mixer. When the dough has come together, turn out onto the work surface and cover with the mixing bowl for 5 minutes.

4. Knead the dough until it is smooth and you can make a gluten window. This should take about 5 minutes. Shape the dough into a smooth ball. Oil a large bowl, and place the dough in the bowl.

5. Spin the dough around the bowl, then flip over so all the sides of the dough have been covered with a bit of oil. Cover with a dish towel or plastic wrap and allow the dough to rise until doubled. This step will take 1 to 1½ hours. The dough should be very puffy and tender to the touch.

6. For cloverleaf rolls, butter/grease two muffin tins.

7. Gently, turn the dough onto a lightly floured work surface. Divide the dough into 24 pieces using a pastry cutter/bench scraper. Then cut each portion into three pieces.

8. Roll each piece between the counter and your palm to create a smooth ball. Place three balls in each muffin cup.

9. Cover the pans with plastic wrap, and allow the rolls to rise. The balls should expand above the top of the pan, and appear as one roll in each cup. This will take 1 to 1½ hours. Be sure to give the rolls enough time to rise. This helps with the fluffy, tender texture. While the rolls are rising, preheat your oven to 350°F.

10. Place the muffin tins in the oven. Bake the rolls until they are golden brown. They may be lighter on the sides, but should be lightly golden on the bottom, approximately 20 to 25 minutes.

11. Remove the pans from the oven. Allow the rolls to rest about 1 to 2 minutes in the pans, then turn out onto a cooling rack.

12. Brush the tops of the rolls with melted butter.

FEEL THE LOVE BREAD STICKS

Makes 32 breadsticks

2 teaspoons(6 grams) active dry yeast

2 cups warm water (105°F)

1½ tablespoons honey

5 tablespoons olive oil, plus more for brushing

5¾ cups (571 grams) all-purpose flour

½ cup Parmesan cheese, grated finely

½ teaspoon garlic powder

4 teaspoon (20 grams) salt

1. Sprinkle the yeast over ½ cup warm water. When the yeast is foamy, add the rest of the ingredients. Mix until shaggy, then turn out on the work surface.

2. Place the mixing bowl over the dough and allow the dough to rest for 5 minutes. Knead the dough until you are able to make a gluten window. Place the dough in a well-oiled bowl. Spin three times and flip.

3. Cover with plastic wrap and allow to rise until doubled in size, about 1 hour.

4. Gently ease the dough from the bowl onto your work surface. Divide into four equal portions. Shape dough into rectangle and divide into eight strips.

5. Cover the dough with a kitchen towel and allow it to rest for 5 minutes, then roll each piece into a long strip, about 16 inches.

6. Place the breadsticks on a parchment-lined baking sheet, cover with a kitchen towel, and allow to rest 30 minutes.

7. While the breadsticks are rising, preheat your oven to 425°F.

8. Before baking, brush breadsticks lightly with olive oil.

9. Bake for 10 to 12 minutes, or until golden brown. For a crunchier breadstick, mist lightly with water before placing them in the oven.

GRISSINI

I love to dip and play with my food. Grissini are fun to eat and great to display in a tall vase on your appetizer table. They're perfect with a glass a wine as your guests arrive.

Makes about 36 long sticks

5 cups (500 grams) all-purpose flour

1 cup warm water (260 grams) 105–110 °F

¼ cup (60 grams) olive oil

3½ tablespoons (50 grams) butter

2 teaspoons (10 grams) salt

1½ tablespoons (15 grams) yeast

¼ cup (50 grams) Parmesan cheese, finely grated

1. Place ½ cup of the warm water in the mixing bowl. Sprinkle the yeast over the water and wait until the mixture is foamy.

2. Add the remaining ingredients, and mix until shaggy. Cover the bowl with a kitchen towel, and allow the dough to rest for 5 minutes.

3. Knead the dough for about 5 minutes, until you can make a gluten window. Place the dough in a well-oiled bowl. Spin three times and flip. Cover with plastic wrap and allow it to rise until it has doubled in size, about 1 hour.

4. Preheat your oven to 375°F. Gently ease the dough from the bowl onto your work surface. Roll into a rectangle 14x16 inches. With a pizza cutter, cut strips about ¼–½ inch wide.

5. Pick up the strips by taking up each end of a strip at the same time, then place the grissini about ¾ to 1 inch apart on a parchment-lined baking sheet. The strips will stretch as you place them.

6. Bake immediately (no need for additional rise) for approximately 10 to 15 minutes, or until golden brown. Allow the grissini to cool, and serve.

chapter five

PASTRIES

story: march to the poubelle

My first course, *Pâtisserie de Base* or Basic Pastry, was in the intensive format, meaning we took three to four classes each day instead of one. It condensed twelve to fourteen weeks of curriculum to just three. It truly was intense. We would be in the lecture room then immediately run downstairs to the kitchen to prepare at least one or all of the recipes the chef had just demonstrated, and then back to the classroom. The days started at 8:00 am and went until 8:00 pm. Some days included a free time block to run an errand, or in our case, to do a little shopping and/or eating. Both activities were highly encouraged. After all, how else were we to learn what great pastries looked and tasted like?

The chefs at Le Cordon Bleu worked a French workweek (35 hours), so we had to have a combination of chefs to cover our long days. Our main pastry chef instructor was off for the evening and bid us farewell. His replacement, who happened to be a Cuisine program chef, was going to oversee our kitchen preparations. All the chefs were very distinguished and impeccably dressed. Our new babysitter chef was even more so. He exuded an air of confidence and importance that had us more nervous than usual. Add to this the rumor that cuisine chefs have little time for pastry chefs (too much weighing and measuring) let alone pastry students in their *first* course.

It was early in the course, and we had seen pastry cream prepared, and made it . . . once. The chef suggested we divide the main recipe and each make a component as if we were working together in a restaurant. One or two people would make a sponge cake, another the mousse, and another the crème pâtissière. This sounded very reasonable. We quickly divided the duties between the members of our small group, carefully increasing the amounts so each of us would have the perfect amount for our individual dessert.

We carefully completed our *mise en place* (gathered our ingredients) and went to work. Our chef walked about the room watching us, helping with any questions, and offering help with locations of ingredients. We had the feeling there were about a million other places he'd rather be, and he had more or less drawn the short straw to teach late that night. Every time he passed by my work station, I got a whiff of his amazing cologne and a stern glance that made me even more nervous. My French was caveman at best, so as he'd pass by, I'd muster a "bonjour Chef" and offer a nice Wisconsin smile. He smiled back, but looked like he had just tasted something sour.

My contribution to our group was the pastry cream. We needed four times the recipe for four students so I had to separate sixteen eggs. It went fine. No broken yolks, and no spills. I gathered the milk, sugar, flour, cornstarch, and eggs and headed over to the stove. I combined the ingredients in the order and technique from my notes and memory. Or so I thought. I stood at the cooktop stirring and stirring, smiling away at the chef as he approached. He stood beside me, and watched me stir. I had nothing to contribute to a conversation so I kept stirring and nervously smiling. Finally, he broke the silence with "Qu'est ce que c'est?" I'm sure I looked at him with a blank, panicked stare. "Qu'est-ce que tu fais?" (what are you making?), he asked. I thought to myself, what is wrong with him? Surely he's seen someone make pastry cream before. "Crème pâtissière, Chef," I said, hoping that he'd move on. But no. Then came the moment. The belly flop in front of your swimming class moment. In one motion, he flicked his head up and to the side, made THE tisk sound, and picked up my saucepan. "Suivez-moi," he said. I looked behind me where my classmates stood paralyzed watching and hoping one could translate. "He wants you to follow him," one piped up. So off we went from one end of the kitchen to the other. It felt like the distance of a football field, but it was really about 50 feet. I was about three steps behind, wondering where we could be going. We arrived at our destination, a gleaming stand holding a perfectly attached garbage bag. Why couldn't we just use the garbage can at our end of the room? He stepped on the foot pedal with his gorgeous French, perhaps Italian, shoes and up went the lid. He stretched out his arms, lifted the pan over his head, and slowly dumped the gooey, wallpaper paste mess from the pan into the garbage. My pastry cream was *poubelle*. Garbage.

"Répétez," he said as he put the pan in a nearby sink. I made the walk of shame back to my workstation. My friends were pale, very sympathetic and trying not to make eye contact. They had busied themselves with things to do that required crouching behind the workstation on the other side. I willed myself not to cry. After all, he didn't yell and scream. But now what? I had no idea what I had done wrong.

"Je vais vous aider à faire de la crème pâtissière," he said. I will help you make pastry cream. I gathered a new set of ingredients. He stood beside the entire time. Part of me wanted to crawl in a hole, and the other part felt like I had a pro at my side that wasn't going to let me screw this up again.

We went to the stove together. I don't know what I did wrong the first time and never will. The second batch required very little time at the stove. "Allez vite," go fast, he said, motioning with his arms so I knew just how fast to go. Our pastry cream was perfect. He held the plastic wrap-lined pan as I plopped the rich, dreamy vanilla custard into the pan. "Vous avez fait un bon travail ce moment." You did a good job that time. No hugs and back slaps, but a slight warmth in his eyes to let me know it was okay.

To this day, I think of him every time I make pastry cream. It's not good, it's great, and I have him to thank. Merci beaucoup, Chef.

I can't stand beside you, but I can walk you through the steps of making crème pâtissière. The perfect pastry cream.

Suggestions jour.

Brique de Chèvre sur Salade

Gratinée aux oignons.

Salade Aveyronnaise
(Confit · Saucisse · Salade H. Vert · Sauce · Tomate.)
Laguiole

Salade Campagnarde.
(Salade · Toast chèvre · Jambon · Emincé · Tomates)

CRÈME PÂTISSIÈRE (PASTRY CREAM)

1 liter milk (whole or 2 percent)

1 vanilla bean, seeds scraped (see Chapter 1)

8 egg yolks from large-sized eggs

1⅓ cups (250 grams) sugar, divided

⅔ cups (60 grams) all-purpose flour

6 tablespoons + 1 teaspoon cornstarch (60 grams)

1. Line a 13x9 inch baking pan with plastic wrap. Make sure the ends of the wrap extend at least 8 to 10 inches past the ends of the pan. Set aside. Be sure you have a space for the pan in your refrigerator. The bottom of the refrigerator is best since it's the coolest. Be sure it's not too close to any perishable items such as mayonnaise.

2. Pour the milk and one half of the sugar into a large saucepan. Add the vanilla seeds and pod. Heat the milk mixture to a low simmer. There should be steam and small bubbles. Using a skimmer or spatula, remove the vanilla bean pod from the milk.

3. While the milk is heating, place the egg yolks in a medium/large bowl. Whisk to loosen. While gently whisking, add the remaining half of the sugar.

4. Whisk until thoroughly combined. Whisk in the flour and cornstarch until combined. The mixture will be stiff.

5. Make sure the pastry cream has your undivided attention. Have your lined pan within reach. This is the grand finale!

6. At the stove, carefully pour one third of the milk into the bowl containing the egg mixture. Whisk/stir well to loosen. Return the saucepan to the heat. Heat briefly to a rolling simmer. Pour the milk/egg mixture from the bowl into the saucepan whisking constantly and very quickly taking care to whisk in the bottom corners of the pan. The mixture will quickly become pastry cream.

7. Whisk over heat just until you see a large bubble "plop" up to the surface. Whisk as you pour the cream into the plastic-lined pan.

8. Cover the pastry cream with the plastic wrap that is extending over the ends of the pan. Place in the refrigerator for at least 3 hours, or until cool throughout.

olive and dexter

Shortly after I started teaching cooking classes, I added birthday party classes for small bakers. Most of the younger children don't bake in class. Instead we decorate small cakes together. Each child decorates a two-layer 6-inch cake. I decorate a big cake for the treat after class. The little 6-inch cakes are filled with icing, stacked together, frosted, decorated more, then placed carefully onto a cake board with a fancy doily then into a real cake box tied with a bow.

Some of my little cake decorators are now high school graduates, college graduates, and are even brides and grooms. Each party has fond memories.

One of my parties didn't involve cake. Meet Olive. She was turning ten years old and didn't have an interest in decorating cakes. She wanted to bake. Not just anything, she wanted to make real French pastries. Her mom and I discussed options and passed a few ideas past Olive. Eclairs were a hit.

The day of the party arrived. Olive and her friends were bright, happy as could be, and adorable. Trailing behind with his dad was Dexter, Olive's little brother. The plan was to have Dexter and his dad go off on an adventure while the girls and mom baked and celebrated the big day. Dexter soon learned of his imminent departure and had other ideas in mind. He quickly dissolved into tears. Weepy to be exact; begging to stay. My heart was melting. The adults were making eye contact trying to think of a plan. Wanting to keep Olive's party little-brother-free, and feeling his pain, I made the proposal. What if Dexter stays and works as my helper? He won't bake with the girls, but he'll stand beside me and help me. Olive seemed okay with the idea, and Dexter was all in. We all put on our aprons, including four-year-old Dexter. As I explained how to make pâté à choux, whipped cream, and pastry cream to the girls, Dexter stood at my side holding spoons, spatulas, and beaming as my class assistant.

The pastries were beautiful. The party was a great success. A few days later an envelope arrived in the mail. It was a note from Dexter in his best four-year-old penmanship. It was many years ago, and I still have his note. We had a great day, and I know I'll remember the day, and I hope he and Olive to do too. Make your own party with some delicious eclairs!

Pâte à Choux

Makes about 24 4–5 inch eclair shells

1 cup (250 grams) water

1 stick minus 1 tablespoon (100 grams) butter, cut into pieces

1⅔ tablespoon (20 grams) sugar

1 teaspoon (5 grams) salt

1½ cups (150 grams) all-purpose flour

4 large eggs

1 batch of Chocolate Glaze (p. 150)

1. Preheat your oven to 375°F.

2. In a medium saucepan, add the water, butter, salt, and sugar. Heat until the butter melts and the water is steamy and at or just about to boil.

3. Turn off the heat for a moment, and add the flour all at once. Place the pan back over low heat. With a wooden spoon (or similar spoon), stir quickly to combine. The mixture will pull completely away from the sides of the pan and looks a lot like mashed potatoes. Continue stirring until a film of dough appears on the bottom of the pan, about 2 to 3 minutes.

4. Transfer the dough to a mixing bowl. Stir in one egg at time. Be sure to incorporate the eggs completely before adding another. Stir until the mixture is smooth and glossy. Be careful not to add all the eggs. You may not need all four. The choux should slowly fall from the spoon, similar to thick lava.

5. Transfer the choux paste to a piping bag fitted with a ½-inch open tip. Line a baking sheet with a silicone mat or parchment paper. Using a ruler or pencil as a guide, pipe ½–¾-inch wide by 4-inch long lines of choux paste.

6. When all the dough has been piped, whisk the remaining egg and brush on the dough. Be very careful not to let the egg drip over the edge of the dough and onto the baking sheet. This may keep the dough from fully puffing in the oven.

7. Then, dip a fork in a cup of water and run the back of the tines gently lengthwise down the dough.

8. Place the baking sheet in the oven and bake for 20 to 25 minutes until the pastry is golden brown. The creases in the pastry should also be golden brown. If under-baked, the puffs can collapse, or be wet and doughy on the inside.

TIP! If you stick your index finger in the dough, swirl it around and pull it out, the dough should hang like a bird's beak off the end of your finger. Most of the time, I only need to add three to three and a half eggs.

The Little French Bakery Cookbook

9. Remove the pastry from the oven and immediately transfer to a wire rack to cool. If you are planning to make eclairs, poke the bottom of the pastry with the end of a clean small paint brush, or skewer in two places, about one third from each end.

10. When cool, fill a pastry bag fitted with a narrow tip. Insert the tip into the holes you made in the bottom and gently fill with cream. Don't overfill. You should just feel a change in the weight of the pastry. Place the pastry back on the wire rack until ready to dip.

11. Prepare the chocolate glaze. Hold the eclair on the side, and press the top into the chocolate. Lift from the chocolate, still upside down, wiping against the edge of the bowl to catch any excess. Carefully turn the eclair over and place in a paper pastry cup or onto a serving platter. Refrigerate until ready to serve. Serve well chilled.

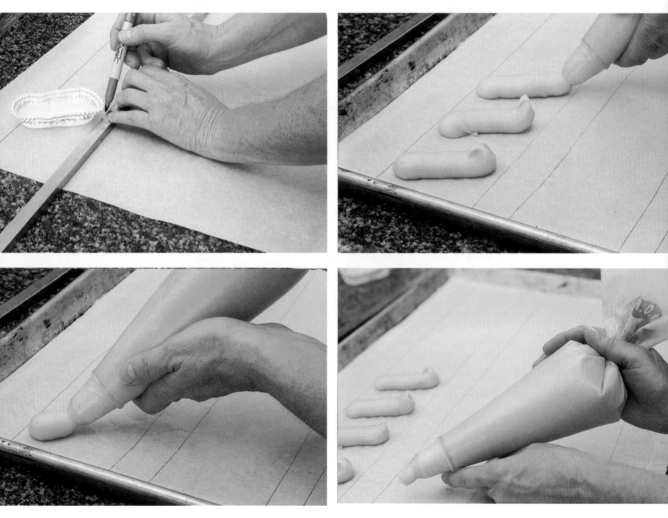

piping technique

The Little French Bakery Cookbook

PROFITEROLES

Profiteroles, small puffs of pâté à choux filled with ice cream then drizzled in warm chocolate sauce, can be found on nearly every dessert menu in France. While the dessert is the same, each restaurant has its own unique way of plating and presenting this delicious treat. The best part for me is seeing how the profiteroles will be served. I love watching the waiter present the puffs accompanied by a beautiful pitcher or carafe containing the molten chocolate sauce. I will never tire of its simple elegance.

1 batch Pâté à Choux (p. 84)

1 pint vanilla bean ice cream, the best you can find

1 batch Chocolate Glaze (p. 150)

1. Slice the puffs crosswise. Fill each puff with a small ball of ice cream. Place three puffs on each plate. Either at the table or before serving, pour the warm glaze over the puffs and serve.

2. If you prefer other flavors of ice cream, substitute your favorite. Coffee, peppermint, or cherry ice cream flavors are a great addition to this wonderful dessert.

LADYFINGER SPONGE CAKE

Ladyfinger sponge cake has a wonderful light, airy texture. It's fun to pipe the batter so it's in one long strip, but looks like you carefully placed individual ladyfingers side by side. You can also make sheet pans of sponge for creating delicious tiramisu. This is one of my favorite classes. Students finish class with beautiful French pastries ready to share with family and friends.

Makes sponge for one mousse cake or 75 ladyfingers

⅔ cup (125 grams) sugar

1¼ cup (125 grams) all-purpose flour

5 large eggs, separated

2–3 tablespoons confectioners' sugar

1. Preheat your oven to 350°F. Line a large baking sheet with parchment paper.

2. Separate the eggs. In a mixing bowl, mix the yolks and about three quarters of the sugar, until the mixture is lightened, and light yellow in color. Set aside.

3. In a separate mixing bowl, add the egg whites and begin whipping with a whisk or the whisk attachment of a stand mixer. When the egg whites have reached soft peaks, add the remaining sugar all at once. Whisk rapidly until the egg whites are shiny and nearly hold firm peaks.

4. With a spatula, fold one quarter of the egg whites in the yolk mixture. Fold in gently. Add another one quarter, and fold. Add the remaining egg whites, and fold until nearly combined. Sprinkle in the flour little by little, gently on the surface, and fold into the eggs. Be careful not to overmix.

5. For ladyfingers, spoon the batter into a large pastry bag fitted with a ½-inch tip. Mark the parchment paper with two parallel lines the length you would like your strip of spongecake. Flip the paper over so you can see the lines through the paper, but aren't piping on the ink. If you are making a mousse cake, draw two circles. One should be about ½ inch smaller than your ring, and the other about 1 to 1½ inches smaller.

6. Pipe ¾-inch strips of batter. Be sure the sides of the strips are touching. With a bit of extra sponge batter, lift the corners of the parchment paper, and place a nickel-sized dollop of batter to secure the paper to the pan. The sponge batter is very light. If you are using a convection oven, the paper will blow off the pan, and onto itself, ruining your ladyfingers. Sift the confectioners' sugar onto the ladyfingers and place in the oven.

7. Bake for 6 to 8 minutes or until the sponge cake is light golden brown and the sponge is also golden on the bottom side when you peek by lifting the corner of the parchment paper. Don't overbake, or the sponge will be too hard to bend into the circle.

8. Remove the sponge (still on the parchment) to a cooling rack, and allow the sponge to cool completely.

For a ladyfinger sheet: Line a jellyroll or half sheet pan with parchment paper. Rather than piping the batter, spread it into the pan. Run your fingers around the edges of the pan to clean any extra batter. Bake as above. The sponge can be removed from the paper using the same technique.

TIP! To remove from the parchment paper, place a second piece of parchment or a clean kitchen towel on your work surface. Lift the parchment with the sponge and place it sponge-side down on the towel. Place a cooling rack on top and lift the baked parchment over the edge of the rack, pulling toward you. As you pull, the rack and parchment will move, and the sponge cake will remain on the work surface. It works every time to keep the sponge from tearing.

Strawberry or Raspberry Mousse Cake (Charlotte)

Makes one Charlotte

One recipe Ladyfinger Sponge Cake

1¼ cup (300 grams) frozen fruit puree

2 tablespoons (30 grams) lemon juice

½ cup (100 grams) sugar or to taste

4–5 gelatin leaves (3¼ teaspoon powdered gelatin)

1 pint (450 grams) heavy cream

Fresh berries for garnish

1. Place the gelatin leaves in cold water to soften. If using powdered gelatin, dissolve in ¼ cup cold water.

2. Whip the cream to medium peaks and place in the refrigerator.

3. Prepare the ladyfinger sponge cake as in the Chocolate Caramel Mousse recipe.

4. In a saucepan, place one half of the fruit puree, lemon juice, and sugar.

5. Heat until the sugar and puree has melted. Squeeze the water from the gelatin leaves and place in the warm mixture. If using powdered gelatin, add the dissolved gelatin and water to the saucepan.

6. Mix well to melt and incorporate the gelatin throughout the mixture. Cool slightly.

7. Place the remaining cold puree in a large bowl. Mash with a fork to break up any large frozen pieces.

8. Add the warm puree mixture to the cold and mix. The mixture should begin to thicken. Allow the mixture to continue to cool (but don't place in refrigerator), until thickened to the texture of loose pudding.

9. Fold in one third of the whipped cream to lighten the mixture. Continue adding and folding in the whipped cream until the mousse is well combined.

10. Spoon the mousse into the ladyfinger ring. Add a layer of sponge trimmings or a disk of sponge cake to help fill the middle, and then fill to the top with the remaining mousse. Smooth with an offset spatula. Or, spoon into small dessert bowls. Garnish with fresh fruit. Place in refrigerator until ready to serve, or 2 hours. This will allow the gelatin to completely set the mousse.

PERFECT WHIPPED CREAM (CREME CHANTILLY)

Whipped cream is one recipe that can be good or really great. To make really great whipped cream, here are some tips.

Start with all of your equipment and cream very cold. I admit, I don't have bowls and whisks living in my refrigerator, just waiting for me to make whipped cream. Instead, I run the mixing bowl and whisks under very cold water, then quickly dry them. Make sure they feel cool to the touch.

The trick to making stable whipped cream with great texture is starting slow, then gradually increasing the speed of whisking.

Is there a difference between machine and hand-whipped cream? I think so. You should try it both ways and see what you think. If you prefer to use a mixer, stop your mixer as the cream looks to be almost finished, then with a large whisk, finish the cream by hand. It won't be more than ten or fifteen whisks, but it will make the cream's texture much better, and I feel a little more stable. The best thing about whipped cream is you can whip it, and then hold it in the refrigerator until you're ready to use it, at least one hour. For mousse recipes, it's one of the things I do first, so I don't have to stop and whip the cream to continue with the recipe.

As I mentioned when talking about equipment, there are several sizes and shapes of whisks. For whipping cream, you'll want to use the biggest whisk you have. Bring out the big balloon whisk if you have one. Choke up on the handle to get a good grip. Work on your technique. When whisking, the whisk should make big circles, not swirl around in the cream. The whisk should come out of the cream, in the air, then down into the cream. Start slowly, and then increase your speed.

Makes about 4 cups

2 cups heavy whipping cream, well chilled

⅓ cup confectioners' sugar

½ teaspoon vanilla extract or favorite liqueur

1. To whip by hand, pour the cream in a large cold bowl. Choke up on the handle of the whisk and begin making big circles, about the size of a large dinner plate. Don't swirl around in the cream. Your whisk should be almost perpendicular to the bowl. Most of the time your whisk will be in the air, then dive down into the cream, adding the air.

2. When the cream is frothy, add the sugar. Slowly increase your speed. As the cream thickens, increase your speed a bit more. It's fine to switch directions and arms. Just keep whisking!

3. Add the vanilla or liqueur as desired. The cream is finished when you have medium soft/firm peaks on the whisk. Store well chilled until ready to use.

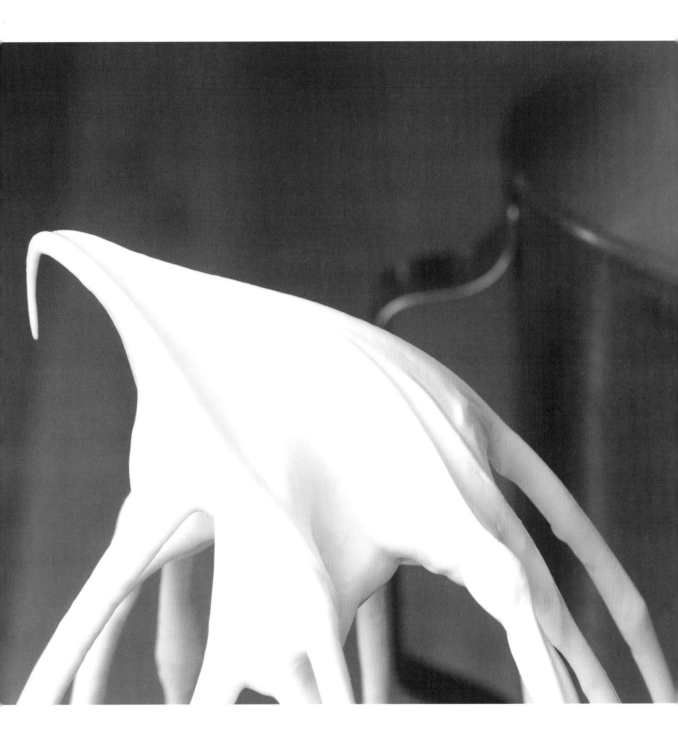

CHOCOLATE CARAMEL MOUSSE

There are many favorite desserts at our house. I would say this one tops the list. It's perfect after any meal. Serve it in individual cups. Or, our favorite is in a big bowl, family style. Pass a little extra whipped cream and some fresh berries. I guarantee the bowl will go around the table at least twice! Unlike some mousse recipes, the eggs in this recipe are fully cooked when combined with the hot caramel, making it very safe.

Makes 8 generous servings

¼ cup (60 grams) water

½ cup minus 1 tablespoon (90 grams) sugar

⅔ cup (150 grams) whipping cream

5 egg yolks (105 grams)

Approx. 1⅛ cup (270 grams) chocolate, chopped (or chips), melted and slightly cooled

2⅓ cups (550 grams) whipping cream

1. Place the yolks in the bowl of a stand mixer or in a large mixing bowl and whisk to loosen.

2. Whip the cream (this time without sugar) and place in the refrigerator until ready to use.

3. In a saucepan, add the water first, then the sugar. Stir to combine. Place over medium heat to cook, not stirring. You will cook until the mixture is a medium amber color. Brush the sides with water if crystals start to form from splashes of sugar on the inside of the pan.

4. At the same time, in another small saucepan, add the whipping cream. Heat the cream to a low simmer.

5. When the caramel has reached the desired color, carefully add the cream. The mixture will spit and sputter. If you place the saucepan above the lower pan, with the handle off to the side, and pour toward you, the pan will protect you from the steam and sputtering. Be very careful to hold your hand away from the top of the saucepan. Stir gently over low heat to dissolve caramel pieces.

> **TIP!** The key to mousse is combining the ingredients at the right temperatures. Be sure the egg and caramel mixture is cool and the chocolate just a bit warm. The egg will help set the chocolate, but you don't want to the chocolate so cool that it hardens and becomes gritty. The mixture should be cool enough so the addition of the cold whipped cream will set the mousse. If the base is too warm the cream will wilt. After the ingredients are combined, you should be able to stand a pastry scraper in the mousse without it tipping over. If it's too thin, spoon rather than pipe into the serving bowl. It will require more chilling time for the mousse to set. The thinner base will be a less airy mousse, but will still taste great.

The Little French Bakery Cookbook

6. Slowly pour the hot caramel over the slowly moving yolks in mixer. Increase the mixer speed and beat until cool. The outside of the mixing bowl should feel cool to the touch.

7. Fold the warm chocolate into cooled egg mixture. Fold in whipping cream.

8. If you're planning to serve the mousse in individual bowls, transfer first, then chill. Or, spoon into a large serving bowl and chill.

TIP! When adding hot sugar into a moving mixer, aim between the side of the bowl and the paddle or whisk attachment. If the sugar or caramel hits the beaters or bowl, it will quickly harden against the sides and be difficult to combine.

MADELEINES

Madeleines instantly take me to Paris. The ingredients are simple and combine to make this sweet little cake. Left open to the air, they'll become crunchy and more like a cookie. I believe the second bite is always the best. Many cafes in France serve a petit madeleine beside your demitasse cup. The waiters at Restaurant Benoit have been known to appear at the end of a meal with a pan of freshly made madeleines—a sweet treat from the kitchen. Look for madeleine pans at your favorite kitchen supply shop.

Makes 24 large or 48 small madeleines

14 tablespoons (200 grams) butter, plus some for buttering the madeleine pans

4 large eggs

¾ cup plus 2 tablespoons (170 grams) granulated sugar

1 pinch salt

½ tablespoon (10 grams) honey

1 teaspoon (5 grams) baking powder

1¾ cup plus 1 tablespoon (180 grams) flour

Confectioners' sugar for dusting

1. Preheat your oven to 350°F. With a pastry brush, brush the pan with softened butter; just in the recessed parts where the madeleines will be. Dust with flour, and tap out any extra.

2. In a clear container, melt the butter and allow to rest until the solids have settled to the bottom.

3. Whisk the sugar and eggs together for at least 5 minutes, until they are light and pale yellow.

4. Add the salt and honey.

5. Fold in baking powder and flour.

6. Carefully pour in the butter, keeping the milk solids back. Fold to combine.

7. Place the bowl in the refrigerator for about 20 minutes to firm the batter.

8. When the batter is cool, spoon it into a pastry bag fitted with a ½-inch open tip. If you don't have one, you can use a plastic zippered bag, with one corner snipped off. Pipe a strip of batter down the center one-third of each indentation.

9. Place in the oven and bake for 6 to 8 minutes or until puffed and golden brown. The madeleines should spring back when lightly touched.

10. Remove the pan(s) from the oven, and immediately rap the edge of the pan on the work surface to knock the cakes from the pan.

11. Transfer them to a cooling rack. If desired, top with sifted confectioners' sugar when cool.

story: you are my favorite chicken

Every August I get a little sentimental. Perhaps more than a little. It brings back memories of arriving in Paris, beginning a journey that would change my life. There's something about the sights and smells of late summer that trigger the memories of walking to the Metro each morning, with excited and nervous butterflies in my stomach. What amazing technique and pastry were we going to learn? Would I be able to understand the chef? And, could I get through the day blunder free?

The day we made Dacquoise in class, it was an evening kitchen session. Our main chef had gone for the day and we had a guest chef from another school. I sound like a broken record, but once again he was very handsome and had even better cologne than the pastry cream chef. To top it off, he wasn't wearing the usual navy blue houndstooth checked pants. His pants were navy blue pin striped. Kim, my classmate and now dear friend, and I secretly called him Fancy Pants. He was very nice, and very helpful.

We gathered our ingredients and proficiently completed the meringue layers. Then came the *cream de beurre*, or buttercream. Since we didn't use mixers, we needed to bring the sugar and water to the soft ball stage, and somehow pour it over the egg yolks waiting in the bowl at our work station, a distance of about 7 feet.

Kim and I had been chatting with the chef (in our best caveman French), trying to be welcoming. While I was bringing my sugar to temp, he walked over to make sure the next step was successful. I remembered earlier in the day that our chef had shown us a way to measure the sugar stage by dipping a flat sieve/skimmer into the sugar and blowing into it. If you can make bubbles, out the back, your sugar is at temp. Amazing. I asked our evening chef about it, and he said, "Oui!" So I gave it a try, and to my amazement, it worked. Now I had sugar at the soft ball stage ready to pour it on the yolks. The chef stood beside me . . . and I froze. "Je poulet, Chef," I said. I wish I could show you the look on his face. Just think about the look a dog gets when you talk to them and they tip their head to the side. Happy, but completely confused. "Poulet?" he said. My friends across the room roared with laughter. I was trying to tell him I was chicken. Guess what? That means nothing in French. One of my French-speaking classmates came to my rescue and explained to the chef that I was afraid to pour the sugar. He smiled and chuckled. I poured the sugar, and began whisking the mixture until it cooled and then added the butter. The buttercream was quite possibly the best thing I had ever tasted. Smooth and rich with the hint of coffee. And best of all, I had just made it.

While we were working, the chef demonstrated how to make marzipan roses using the back of a tablespoon. In addition, he made a few small animals, often seen in patisserie cases.

We assembled our desserts and presented them to the chef for grading. As we were boxing our dessert and preparing for the Metro ride back to the hotel, the chef walked up beside me, and with the biggest smile, set a little marzipan chicken on my workstation. "You are my favorite Chicken," he said.

"Merci, Chef," I replied and I'm sure blushed six shades of red. I still teach students how to make roses, Dacquoise, and buttercream. And best of all, when Kim and I are together we often reminisce about Fancy Pants.

I've been wanting to share this recipe for a long time. It's an incredible dessert. It's pure classic French pastry. Simple ingredients combined together to make each component. Combined together, you won't believe how elegant and delicious it tastes.

Dacquoise is a nut-based meringue sponge cake, which makes it naturally gluten-free if that's important for you. You can use all almonds, hazelnuts, or a mixture. The key is to make great egg whites.

> **TIP!** For the very best meringue, start with eggs whites at room temperature or just a bit above. Start whipping them slowly, then gradually increase the speed. Once they reach soft peaks, add the sugar all at once and increase the mixer speed (or find a new set of arms if you're whisking by hand), and whisk until the peaks are firm and shiny.

Dacquoise

Makes two 10-inch circles

9 egg whites

2¼ cups (340 grams) almond and/or hazelnut flour

1 dash salt

1 dash cream of tartar

1½ cups (300 grams) granulated sugar

1. Preheat your oven to 350°F.

2. Line baking sheet with parchment paper.

3. Bring the egg whites, cream of tartar, and salt to soft peaks. Add the sugar and increase speed until egg whites become medium firm with glossy peaks.

4. Fold in the nut flour.

5. Spread in the rings, or spread in the circle, about ½–¾ inch thick.

6. Bake for 30 minutes, until golden brown. The Dacquoise will rise and then settle back into the ring.

7. Cool completely.

8. Peel off the parchment paper, and carefully remove from the rings. To finish the dessert, use a thin knife with the blade pointed toward the edge of the pan, and carefully cut the cake away from the edge.

9. Place on a plate, and pipe several rosettes of buttercream. Be sure to pipe a ring of rosettes near the edge. Set the next layer on top and garnish with more rosettes of buttercream. If you have some chocolate coffee beans, or nuts, add one to each rosette.

CREME DE BEURRE (FRENCH BUTTERCREAM)

4 egg yolks, from large-sized eggs

14 tablespoons (200 grams) butter, at room temperature

1 cup (230 grams) water

1⅓ cups (170 grams) confectioners' sugar

1. In a mixing bowl or the bowl of a standing mixer, have the egg yolks ready. Be sure the butter is at room temperature. In a small saucepan, add the water, then add the sugar and heat to 238°F. Use a candy thermometer to check the temperature.

2. When the sugar/water reach soft ball stage, slowly pour it over yolks, whisking continuously. Continue whisking by hand or with the whisk of the mixer, until the mixture is cool. If you feel the bottom of the bowl, you'll feel that the mixture is cool.

3. Add the butter 1 to 2 tablespoons at a time, incorporating well after each addition. If the mixture breaks, keep mixing. It will come back together. Add the coffee extract to taste, about 2 to 3 teaspoons. The buttercream should be a rich coffee color, with a nice coffee taste.

TIP! Be sure your butter is at room temperature. Buttercream is much easier with a mixer, but it can definitely be done by hand with a whisk. You may need a helper to hold the bowl while you whisk in the hot sugar so your bowl doesn't scoot away.

The Little French Bakery Cookbook

FRENCH COFFEE EXTRACT (ESSENCE DE CAFE)

1 cup (200 grams) granulated cane sugar

7 ounces (200 grams) water

¼ pound or 1⅞ cup (100 grams) instant coffee, Nescafe is my favorite

1. Dissolve the instant coffee in the water and bring to a boil, then reduce to a simmer. In another saucepan, cook the sugar until very dark caramel color (very dark amber).

2. Stop the caramel by adding the hot coffee. The mixture will bubble, spit, and sputter. Be very careful to protect your hands and fingers. Add the coffee slowly, and stir lightly to dissolve any hard caramel bits.

3. Strain the mixture and cool.

4. Pour into bottles, and store in refrigerator.

mariage frères is a wonderful stop for a cup of tea and pastry.

WEEKEND POUND CAKE

Makes one pound cake

6 large eggs

1¼ cups sugar (240 grams)

2½ cups minus 1 tablespoon flour (340 grams)

1½ cups or 3 sticks melted butter (340 grams)

½ teaspoon vanilla extract

Zest of one lemon

Juice of one lemon

Apricot glaze (nappage), or apricot preserves heated and strained to remove solids

1 cup confections' sugar

1 tablespoon water

1. Melt butter and let milk solids drift and settle to the bottom of the container. Using melted butter and a pastry brush, carefully butter the small bread pans. Take special care in the corners. Turn upside down to allow butter to set and not pool in bottom.

2. Whisk flour or pass through sieve or sifter.

3. Combine eggs and sugar; add lemon zest and vanilla. Whip by hand or with a stand mixer fitted with the whisk attachment until the mixture gently falls from the whisk in a ribbon, then sets on the surface before fading into the mixture. This is called the ribbon stage. The mixture will be light, pale yellow, and creamy.

4. Gently fold in flour about one third at a time. When all the flour has been added, add butter slowly without adding milk solids that have settled on the bottom. Fill your pans about three fourths full and bake in 350°F oven for about 40 minutes or until done or when a toothpick inserted into the center comes out clean.

5. Turn the loaves out of pans immediately. Place on cooling rack.

6. Prepare the glaze with water and powdered sugar and 2 teaspoons lemon juice, set aside. When the cakes are cool, brush nappage/apricot glaze over entire cakes.

7. Place in refrigerator to allow the glaze to set. Brush with sugar glaze. Set in warm but cooling oven for just a few moments to set sugar glaze. Slice and garnish with fresh berries as desired.

SWISS MERINGUE

French pastries, breads, and ice creams require many eggs yolks. Pastry chefs, not wanting to waste egg whites, make meringue at the end of the day. When the baking for the day is complete, the meringue goes into the oven to bake in the warm, cooling oven. The beautiful meringue is ready when the baker returns. You'll find these pillowy clouds of meringue as you enter many patisseries.

8 egg whites (from large-sized eggs)
2⅔ cups (500 grams) granulated sugar, preferably cane sugar

1. Line a baking sheet with parchment paper.
2. Prepare a *bain marie*, or double boiler, by adding water to a large saucepan or sauté pan about one quarter full. Heat water to a simmer. In another bowl, which will fit over or into the bain marie, add the eggs and sugar. If you are going to be using a stand mixer, use the mixer's bowl.
3. Whisk together the eggs and sugar, then place the bowl over the pan of barely simmering water. Heat the egg/sugar mixture to 50–60°C or 122–140°F.
4. Whisk continuously, or as much as you can since you'll need to stop to check temperatures. It will take about 15 to 20 minutes for the sugar/egg mixture to heat. It will be thick and syrupy, not fluffy yet. If you are using a stand mixer, carefully place the bowl on the mixer with the whisk attachment.
5. Begin whipping mixture until nearly cool and very light and fluffy. This will take about 15 to 20 minutes, though it can take longer. Be careful not to overbeat the meringue. It will become grainy. When the meringue is ready, you may wish to add a few drops of food coloring.
6. While the meringue is whipping, preheat your oven to 200°F. If your oven has convection function either turn it off the feature or reduce the heat by 25°F. It is better to bake a little cooler than too warm.
7. Transfer the meringue into a pastry bag fitted with a large open or star tip. Pipe a 3–4 inch flat base, extending the edges up with one more round to make a cup shape. You can also use a spoon to drop the meringue onto the parchment-lined sheet and shape the cups with the back of the spoon.
8. Place the pan in the center of oven. Bake for about 2 hours, or until the cups remove easily from the parchment paper. They should be crisp and light without any browning. Once the meringue cups have finished baking, you can turn off the oven and cool the cups in the oven. This will help them stay crisp and bake completely.

TIP! To separate egg whites, use cold fresh eggs. Eggs separate more easily if they are cold. Be sure there are no bits of broken yolks in the egg whites. To help keep the yolk from breaking, crack the egg on a flat surface rather than on the edge of the bowl. After cracking, open the egg into the open palm of your hand. The white will run between your fingers and the yolk will stay intact in your hand. Gently roll the yolk into the bowl. Whites will whip better if they are at room temperature or warmer. Set the bowl containing your egg whites over another bowl of warm water. Swish them around in the bowl and the chill will disappear. Your egg whites will be perfect.

MUSHROOMS, KISSES, AND FAIRY FINGERS

Rather than piping cups, pipe small domes and kiss shapes and bake. The dome can be "glued" to the top of the kiss point to make a mushroom with melted chocolate. Dust with cocoa.

For fairy fingers, add a few drops of pink food coloring and pipe thin strips. "Glue" these strips together with jam.

SCHAUM TORTE

Makes 4–6 meringue cups

1 pint strawberries, hulled
    and sliced
½ cup granulated sugar

1 pint vanilla ice cream
1 tablespoon Grand Marnier or
    orange liqueur (optional)

1. Place berries in bowl, sprinkle with sugar, and toss to combine. Allow to rest about 1 hour. The sugar will macerate the berries, creating more juice.

2. Mash the berries slightly and sprinkle with liqueur.

3. Top the meringues with vanilla ice cream then strawberries. Be sure to drizzle with some of the strawberry juices.

JUMBO MARSHMALLOWS

Once you've mastered eggs whites and soft ball stage sugar, the next step is marshmallows. These need to rest overnight, so be sure to start them the day ahead of your plans. I like this recipe because the gelatin is added later in the process, and requires less beating. Your mixer will thank you! This recipe was adapted from *Living the Sweet Life in Paris*, by David Lebovitz.

Makes about 24 to 36 large marshmallows

2 envelopes powdered gelatin, or 17–18 grams gelatin leaves (about 8–10 sheets)

½ cup cold water for dissolving gelatin (or 2 cups cold water for leaves)

⅓ cup cold water for heating sugar

1 cup (200 grams) granulated sugar

⅓ cup (100 grams) light corn syrup

4 egg whites (from large eggs)

Pinch of salt

2 teaspoons vanilla extract or ½ teaspoon vanilla paste

Marshmallow dusting powder (1 cup cornstarch mixed with 1 cup powdered sugar)

Cooking spray

1. Spray a 13x9 inch baking pan with cooking spray and dust with dusting powder. Shake out any excess. Make sure the entire inside of the pan is covered.

2. In a small bowl dissolve the gelatin in cold water.

3. In a saucepan, combine the ⅓ cup water, corn syrup, and granulated sugar.

4. Heat the sugar to 240°F. While the sugar is heating, place the egg whites in the bowl of a stand mixer (fitted with the whisk) with a pinch of salt. Begin whipping the egg whites. You'll want the egg whites to reach medium soft peaks as the sugar reaches the soft ball stage.

5. When the sugar is just over 240°F (nearing 245°F), pour the syrup over the egg whites. Keep the eggs moving. Try to avoid hitting the whisk with the syrup. It will splatter and stick to the sides of the bowl.

6. With the same saucepan, add the gelatin. If you are using gelatin leaves, squeeze out the water and add the gelatin to the saucepan. Add 2 tablespoons of the soaking water to the gelatin. If you're using powdered gelatin, add it to the saucepan. Heat the gelatin until it has dissolved.

7. Pour the warm gelatin over the egg mixture.

8. Continue beating the marshmallow mixture for about 5 to 8 minutes or until the outside of the bowl feels cool to the touch. The marshmallow should be billowy but not too sticky or stiff.

9. Spread the marshmallow into the prepared pan. Use a spatula to smooth the surface. Allow the pan to rest uncovered for 2 hours.

10. Dust the top of the marshmallow with more dusting powder, and dry uncovered overnight.

11. Turn the marshmallow out onto a piece of parchment paper. Cut into squares or other shapes using a scissors, pizza cutter, or cookie cutter.

12. Place the remaining dusting powder in a large zip-top plastic bag or bowl. Toss the marshmallows in the dusting powder to coat.

13. Store marshmallows in an airtight container for about 1 week.

CROISSANTS AND PAIN AU CHOCOLAT

It was about midway though our first pastry course. One day, toward the end of a class, the chef asked us to combine the list of ingredients you see below and place it in the refrigerator overnight. "Demain, nous allons faire des croissants" he said. I couldn't believe my ears. After several classes and days of new desserts, we were going to make croissants. I was beyond excited.

The next day we went to our demonstration and watched him prepare not only croissants but pain au chocolate, pain au raisin, and croissant amande (almond). At the end of the class, we were were offered a few bites. They were the best croissants I had ever tasted. Was it really possible we would be able to reproduce pastries like this in just a few minutes?

Class ended, and we climbed the six flights of stairs to the kitchen. It was a gorgeous day. The sun was streaming in the windows onto the shiny marble work station. In France, there aren't screens on the windows, which somehow made the sunshine feel even more special.

I pulled my dough from the refrigerator, prepared my butter, and followed the step-by-step instructions under the close supervision of our chef. Just as I was about to cut my croissants, I looked down at the flour-covered surface and the beautiful dough. It hit me. I was really in Paris, at Le Cordon Bleu, about to cut my first croissants. I willed myself not to cry, and ducked under the counter to where we kept our notebooks, utensils, and cameras. I had to capture this moment.

Through my misty eyes, I snapped a photo of my dough with the open window in the background. This was the predigital camera era so I had to wait for my photos to be developed. When I got back the developed photo, it didn't look like anything too special. Croissant dough on marble. Yet every time I see the photo I'm reminded of the moment like it was yesterday.

This is one of the most requested classes. It took me years to figure out a way to teach all the steps in one day. I prepare the first part for the class the day before, then the students fold in the butter and create pastries in class. I always hope they enjoy their first experience with the beautiful dough as much as I did.

Makes about 15 croissants or pain au chocolat

For the Dough:

6 cups all-purpose flour (600 grams)

2 teaspoons salt (10 grams)

⅓ cup sugar (56 grams)

1 tablespoon instant yeast

6½ oz milk (200 grams)

1 cup water

2 tablespoons soft butter

For the Folding Butter:

3 sticks cold (1½ cups) unsalted butter, the best you can find

2 tablespoons flour

1 egg for brushing the croissants

Chocolate batons or bittersweet chocolate pieces for pain au chocolat

1. With a stand mixer fitted with the paddle or by hand, mix the ingredients (except cold butter and 2 tablespoons flour) until shaggy.

2. Gently knead for 1 to 2 minutes until smooth. Dough will be sticky. Place in lightly oiled bowl covered with plastic wrap and chill overnight.

3. The next day, cut the folding butter into ½-inch pieces, sprinkle with the 2 tablespoons flour, and pound between two pieces of parchment with a rolling pin or beat in mixer with flour until smooth. Be sure to keep the butter cool. Shape into a 6x6 inch square about ½ inch thick. Return to the refrigerator if your butter feels too soft.

4. Place the dough on your lightly floured work surface. Roll the dough into a 7x14 inch rectangle. Start with the narrow edge nearest to you. Place the butter square on the bottom half of the dough, and fold the top half over the butter. Lightly seal the edges, and tap with the rolling pin to even out the thickness.

TIP! Be sure you can always slide the dough easily on the work surface. If the dough sticks, the butter will break out of the dough. But be careful not to dust with too much flour. Use a dry pastry brush or big flour brush to brush away any excess flour on the dough as you continue.

---

5. Turn the dough one-quarter turn so the fold is on the left and could open like a book.

6. Roll the dough, keeping about the same width, to 24 inches in length. Fold the dough into thirds, as you would a letter. Tap the dough to even the thickness, and turn again so the fold is on the left side. You've just completed one turn!

7. Cover the dough lightly with plastic wrap and rest at room temperature for 20 minutes. If your room is warmer than 72°F, and you have concern about the dough becoming too soft, you can also rest the dough in the refrigerator.

8. Make two more turns (waiting at least 20 minutes between turns). Remember, if your room isn't too warm, you don't need to return to the refrigerator after each turn. Each time you fold the dough, you're making more and more layers of butter and dough. When the butter heats and melts in the oven, the water in the butter will become steam. The steam pushes the layers of dough apart creating the flaky light layers of the croissants.

9. For croissants, divide the dough into two portions. Roll the first piece of dough into a 6x18 inch rectangle. Cut triangles with a bottom width of about 3 inches. Roll the triangle to lengthen, cut a ½-inch slit on the bottom edge. Starting at the bottom, roll the dough towards the point, gently stretching the dough. Use both hands, splaying them apart as you roll. The slit will help widen the dough and create a traditional shape. It will take about three to four rolls to reach the end. Place the croissants on a parchment-lined baking sheet, point side down. Repeat with the second portion of dough.

10. For pain au chocolat, cut rectangles measuring 3x4 inches. Place a chocolat baton at each end. Roll/fold each end of the dough toward the center, then each end once again. This will create a scroll shape. Place the dough smooth side up, rolls down, on the baking sheet.

11. When finished shaping, cover and allow the pastries to rise at room temperature for 1 hour. While the dough is rising, preheat your oven to 350°F. Just before baking, beat the egg in a small bowl with a fork. With a pastry brush, gently brush the tops of the croissants with egg wash. Try not to let the egg to drip down the sides of the croissant onto the pan.

12. Bake at 350°F, for 30 minutes. Rotate pan half way through if necessary. Transfer pan to a cooking rack, and allow pastries to cool at least 30 minutes. If you serve the croissants too soon, the butter will not have cooled, and the pastry will have a greasy feel and taste.

TIRAMISU

This Italian classic is a favorite of many Little French Bakery customers. I make the ladyfinger sheets from scratch every time. Now you can too. Pasteurized egg yolks are now readily available in the dairy sections of groceries. You can make the ladyfinger sponge cake one day, and assemble the next day. Allow for the assembled tiramisu to set/chill for at least six to eight hours or overnight before serving.

Makes one 13x9 inch pan

2 batches of ladyfinger sponge cake

⅓ cup pasteurized egg yolks (or egg substitute)

1 pound mascarpone cheese

⅔ cup granulated sugar

3–3½ gelatin sheets (or 1 envelope gelatin powder)

¼ cup brandy

1 cup whipping cream

For the Imbibing Liquid:

1 pint Irish Cream liqueur

1½ cups heavy cream

¼ cup strong coffee or espresso, cooled

1. Place the gelatin sheets in cold water. If using powdered gelatin, sprinkle over ⅛ cup cold water.

2. Place the eggs and sugar in a mixing bowl fitted with a whisk attachment and beat until light and pale yellow. Add the cheese and beat until light and combined.

3. Squeeze the liquid from the gelatin sheets. Heat the brandy over low heat, add the gelatin sheets or dissolved powdered gelatin. Stir to melt/dissolve. Cool slightly and add to the mascarpone mixture.

4. Add the cold heavy whipping cream and whip until light, with medium firm peaks.

5. Combine the imbibing syrup.

6. Remove the parchment from the sponge cake. Divide each piece in half. If you had to bake in another sized pan, cut pieces to create three 13x9 pieces.

7. In a 13x9 inch baking pan, place a layer of sponge cake. With a pastry brush, soak the sponge cake with the imbibing liquid. Be generous!

8. Spread one third of the whipped mascarpone mixture over the sponge cake. Repeat with two more layers of sponge and mascarpone mixture, ending with the whipped mixture on top. Be sure to imbibe the sponge cake well.

9. Place a piece of plastic wrap against the surface of the cream, and chill.

10. When ready to serve, dust with cocoa and grated chocolate. Cut 3x3 inch squares and place on a plate dusted with cocoa. It's easiest to cut with a knife dipped in warm water. Garnish with more grated chocolate.

TIP! If you have a bar of chocolate, use a peeler on the edge to make pretty chocolate curls and shavings for an extra special garnish.

ENGLISH TRIFLE

A trifle is a wonderful dessert when celebrating with a large group. Our friends Stacy and Steve order a trifle every Christmas Eve for their family dinner. Over the years, we've perfected just the right amount of "boozy," a favorite food term of Julia Child for imbibing liqueur into dessert. Trifle bowls are available in every price category from discount department stores to famous crystal designers. The tall sides of the bowl show off the layers and contrast of the cake and fruit.

For the trifle sponge cake:

¾ cup unsalted butter, softened

1 cup (200 grams) granulated sugar

3 large eggs

2 cups (200 grams) all-purpose flour

4 teaspoons baking powder

For the custard:

1 recipe Creme Pâtissiere (pastry cream), loosened

1 tablespoon Grand Marnier or Cointreau to flavor pastry cream as desired

4–6 cups assorted berries (frozen berries work great)

1 cup good quality raspberry preserves

½ cup Sherry

2 cups heavy whipping cream, whipped and chilled

1 cup sliced almonds, lightly toasted

For the trifle sponge cake:

1. Preheat oven to 350°F. Butter and flour two 8-inch cakes pans, or one 12-inch round pan and line with parchment paper.

2. In a food processor, cream butter and granulated sugar for 1 minute.

3. With motor running, add eggs one at a time and process for 5 seconds after each addition.

4. Sift flour and baking powder together and add to bowl or processor. Pulse to fold in flour. Just a few pulses. Don't over work the batter. Your batter will be very stiff.

5. Spread the batter in the pan or divide between the two pans.

6. Bake 20 to 30 minutes, until golden and when a toothpick inserted into the center comes out clean.

7. Cool completely. The cake will be very dry and firm to the touch.

For the custard:

1. Prepare the pastry cream and cool completely in the refrigerator. When ready to assemble the trifle, loosen the pastry cream by placing it in a medium bowl and whisking firmly. When the cream has a smooth consistency, whisk in the liqueur, if desired. A stand mixer fitted with the paddle attachment does an excellent job with this step. Be sure not to add the liqueur too soon or your cream may be a bit lumpy.

2. Remove the cakes from the pan(s). You may need to run a butter knife around the edge of the pan. Flip the pan over and gently rap on the work surface. The cake with the parchment will drop from the pan. It works well to have a clean sheet of parchment paper on your work surface.

The Little French Bakery Cookbook

3. Spread a generous layer of preserves on the cakes, then cut into 1-inch cubes.

4. In a trifle bowl, or large clear bowl, place half of the cake cubes. Generously sprinkle with the Sherry.

5. Layer half of the pastry cream over the cake. Sprinkle generously with Sherry.

6. Layer about 2 cups of fruit over the pastry cream. Don't worry about the juices. As the fruit thaws it will add a lovely flavor and juice to the cream and cake.

7. Repeat with another layer of cake, cream, and fruit, sprinkling with Sherry with each addition.

8. You should be near the top of your trifle bowl.

9. Cover firmly with plastic wrap and refrigerate until you're ready to serve and display your trifle.

10. While the trifle is chilling, toast the almonds by placing them in a small skillet over medium heat. Toss constantly until they reach a pretty golden color and have a nice almond smell. You can also place them on a baking sheet and bake at 350°F until they are golden. Check them often, and toss with a spatula to prevent them from burning.

11. When you're ready to serve the trifle, whip the cream to medium peaks. Add to the top of the trifle in pretty spoonfuls, or pipe through a pastry bag with a large star tip. Add the almonds, and serve using a big spoon. The pastry cream is perishable, so be sure to keep the trifle well chilled until ready to serve.

LEMON CHEESECAKE WITH BERRIES

In 1983, my dad had coronary bypass surgery. I was waiting in the surgical waiting area with my mom. We were thumbing through magazines passing the time. A recipe in *Gourmet* magazine caught my eye—a recipe for lemon cheesecake. I was 23 years old, living with roommates, and had never tried to make a cheesecake. I copied down the recipe, and a week or so later made my very first cheesecake. It was tough using a little hand mixer to get the cream cheese mixed with the other ingredients. My parents heard of my dilemma and presented me with a new mixer on my birthday. It could be a hand mixer or oscillate on its stand. It was wonderful. A springform pan, and a mixer capable of mixing all the ingredients together made the next preparation of the recipe a dream. I've made the cheesecake many times over the years. It's fun to add new flavorings and use other crusts. Here's the recipe that started it all. It has a creamy, firm texture. It's adapted from The Old Rittenhouse Inn's recipe. The Inn is a wonderful landmark in northern Wisconsin.

Makes one 10-inch cheesecake

For the crust:

2 cups (200 grams) all-purpose flour

Zest of one lemon

½ pound (2 sticks) unsalted butter, cut into ½ inch pieces

2 large eggs yolks

1 teaspoon vanilla extract

For the filling:

2½ pounds cream cheese (any assortment of full or low fat), at room temperature

1¾ cups (336 grams) granulated sugar

Zest of one lemon

1 teaspoon vanilla extract

2 tablespoons all-purpose flour

1 teaspoon salt

4 large eggs

2 large egg yolks

¼ cup heavy cream

For the topping:

⅓ cup granulated sugar

⅓ cup water

1 tablespoon light corn syrup

4 teaspoons corn starch

3–4 cups fresh or frozen berries

For the crust:

1. Preheat your oven to 400°F.

2. In a bowl, using a pastry cutter, blend the butter, sugar, and lemon zest together. The mixture should be like sand. You can use a food processor or mixer. Be sure to work in small bursts to create a sandy mixture rather than dough. Add the egg yolks and vanilla. Quickly mix together. The dough should be cool to the touch and smooth.

3. Remove the ring from a 10-inch springform pan. Press one third of dough onto the bottom of the springform pan. It will resemble shortbread dough. Place the bottom of the pan directly on the oven rack, bake for 6 to 8 minutes, until the dough is light golden.

4. Remove from the oven and cool on a wire rack. When the bottom is cool enough to handle, attach the ring to the pan and press the remaining dough onto the sides of the pan, about 2 inches high. Be sure to extend the side down onto the bottom to create a good seam. Try to make the dough the same thickness, with a nice clean edge at the top. The dough will be about ¼ inch thick. Set the pan aside.

For the Cheesecake filling:

1. Increase the oven temperature to 425°F.

2. In a large bowl (or the bowl of a stand mixer), beat the cream cheese until it's smooth, scraping the bowl once or twice.

3. Add the sugar, zest, salt, and vanilla. Beat well to combine.

4. Add the eggs and yolks one at a time, beating to combine and scraping the bowl after each addition.

5. Add the flour and beat to combine. Scrape the bowl, and add the heavy cream. Beat to combine. The mixture should be very smooth and light.

6. Pour the filling into the crust. Smooth the top with a spatula.

7. Set the pan on a baking sheet lined with parchment paper. This will catch any drips from the springform pan. Place the pan in the center of the oven. Bake for 15 minutes, then reduce the oven temperature to 300°F.

8. Bake for an additional 60 minutes. The cheesecake will be mostly set, but may jiggle in the center. Remove the cheesecake from the oven and carefully transfer to a wire rack. Cool on the rack for 20 minutes, then open the clasp on the springform pan, but don't remove it completely.

9. Allow the cheesecake to cool for another 45 minutes, then transfer to the refrigerator to cool completely (springform ring still in place, but slightly open).

For the topping:

1. In a small saucepan, combine the water, sugar, and cornstarch. Heat to a boil. The mixture will become slightly clear and thicken.

2. Add the corn syrup. Fold in the berries. Allow the mixture to cool, then spoon onto the top of the cheesecake.

Variations:

Chocolate Swirl:

Omit the lemon zest. Divide the cheesecake filling into two thirds and one third. In the one third, add ½ cup cocoa and mix well. Pour the two-thirds filling into the crust. Using a tablespoon, spoon the chocolate mixture onto the filling leaving 1-inch spaces between the spoonfuls of chocolate. With a butter knife, drag the knife through the filling in a figure eight motion to swirl the filling. Don't overmix so the filling combines. Bake as directed.

Key Lime:

Omit the lemon zest. Add ¼ cup key lime juice to the filling. Bake as directed.

Pumpkin:

Omit the lemon zest. Add ¾ cup pumpkin puree (not pumpkin pie filling), add ½ teaspoon ground clove, 1 teaspoon cinnamon, and ½ teaspoon ground ginger. For a great topping, mix 1½ cups sour cream and ¼ cup granulated sugar. About 10 minutes before the cheesecake finishes, pour mixture onto the top and continue baking. Garnish with toasted pecans.

Salted Caramel Apple Cheesecake Tart

When the weather turns cool and fall is in the air, there's nothing better than caramel and apples. Paired with cheesecake and a crunchy graham crust, you'll have just the dessert for an autumn dinner or pumpkin carving party.

Serves 8 to 10

For the crust:

1 package graham crackers (about 12 full crackers) crushed into crumbs

3 tablespoons unsalted butter, melted

¼ teaspoon salt

½ teaspoon vanilla extract

¼ cup granulated sugar

For the cheesecake filling:

1 pound cream cheese (any assortment of full or low fat), at room temperature

1 cup (192 grams) granulated sugar

1 teaspoon vanilla extract

1 tablespoon all-purpose flour

½ teaspoon salt

2 large eggs

1 large egg yolk

2 tablespoons heavy cream or sour cream

1–2 Golden Delicious or Granny Smith apples

1–2 tablespoons granulated sugar (for sprinkling on the apples)

a few dashes of cinnamon

For the caramel layer:

1½ cups (288 grams) granulated sugar

½ cup water

1 cup heavy cream

½ cup (96 grams) granulated sugar

2 tablespoons unsalted butter

Sea salt flakes for garnish

1. Preheat your oven to 350°F. Line an 8-inch round cake pan lined with foil. The foil should extend slightly over the edge of the pan. Spray the foil with cooking spray or lightly oil.

2. Mix all the crust ingredients together until they feel like wet sand. Press into the bottom of the cake pan. Bake for 10 minutes, remove, and cool while you prepare the filling. Keep your oven on.

3. With a mixer, beat the cream cheese to loosen, then add the sugar. Beat until smooth. Be sure to scrape the bowl to combine well.

4. Add the eggs, one at a time, mixing well after each addition. Add the cream, salt, flour, and vanilla and beat. Pour the cheesecake mixture onto the crust.

5. Peel and core the apple. Cut the apple in half top to bottom, then make thin slices (vertically is easiest). Try to make the slices all one thickness if you can. Layer the slices on top of the cheesecake in two concentric rings. Sprinkle with sugar and cinnamon.

6. Place in the oven and bake for 15 minutes. Reduce the oven heat to 300°F and bake for an additional 15 minutes or until the cheesecake feels firm to the touch. If apples begin to brown too much, cover the pan with foil.

7. Remove from the oven to a cooling rack while you prepare the caramel.

8. In a deep saucepan, add the water and the sugar. Heat over medium/high heat. At the same time, in another saucepan, heat the cream and ½ cup sugar to a simmer.

9. Continue cooking the sugar and water mixture without stirring until the mixture is a medium amber caramel color. Carefully pour the cream mixture into the caramel. Add the cream with caution. The mixture will bubble, sputter, and steam. Stir gently to dissolve any caramel bits. When the bubbling has subsided, transfer the caramel into a heat-proof bowl. Stir in the butter 1 tablespoon at a time.

10. Pour the caramel onto the apples in a thin layer. You will not use all the caramel. Reserve some for drizzling at the table. Allow the dessert to cool completely. Lift the tart from the pan using the foil to lift. Gently peel the foil away from the sides and slide a plate under the crust.

11. When ready to serve, sprinkle with sea salt flakes. Store the cheesecake in the refrigerator.

TARTE TATIN

There are certain pastries I seek out whenever I'm in Paris. Tarte Tatin is one of them. As the story goes, the Tatin sisters operated a hotel. While preparing tarts for the upcoming meal, one sister overcooked the apples so she added the crust to the top of the apples still in the pan and placed it in the oven. The result is an apple upside-down tart. The apples are cooked and caramelized before placing the tart crust over the top.

The Golden Delicious apples are tender and delicious. The pastry is as beautiful as it is delicious. Serve it in generous wedges with a dollop of crème fraîche or ice cream.

Makes one Tarte Tatin

1 recipe Pâte Brisée
¾ cup (150 grams) granulated sugar
9 tablespoons (about 4.5 oz) unsalted butter, melted
3 pounds Golden Delicious apples, peeled and cored

1. In a Tarte Tatin pan, or a 9-inch round baking pan with tall sides, such as a cake pan, add the butter and sugar.

2. Peel and core the apples, then cut in half, top to bottom. Place the apples (on end) in the sugar, being sure to pack them in tightly since the apples will shrink. Place the outer edge of the apple pieces against the edge of the pan if possible.

3. Preheat your oven to 350°F. Place the pan on the stovetop over medium-high heat.

4. Cook until the apples' juices have almost evaporated, and caramel is forming in the bottom of the pan. Depending on the apples, you may need to spoon off some liquid during the cooking process. Try not to disturb the apples. This may take 30 to 40 minutes.

5. When the juices have mostly evaporated, and the caramel is just light golden, roll the pâte brisée into a 10-inch circle.

6. When the sugar has begun to caramelize, place the dough on top of the apples. Trim and turn edges to create a decorative edge. The pan and sugar will be very hot. Be very careful. You may only be able to trim the dough. It will still be pretty!

7. Place the pan on a parchment-lined baking sheet to catch any drips of juice or caramel from the pan. Bake for approximately 30 minutes, or until the crust is golden.

8. Remove the pan from the oven, and cool 1 to 2 minutes. Place a serving platter over the crust, then flip quickly to turn the Tarte Tatin apple side up. Lift off the pan. Serve immediately with crème fraîche or ice cream.

chapter six

COOKIES AND BARS

CRANBERRY OATMEAL CHIP COOKIES

In Wisconsin, we have an abundance of dried cranberries. This cookie makes a great treat for a gift to someone special. Make extra—you'll love them too. While much like the Kitchen Sink Cookie, this cookie uses butter rather than shortening. Create your own twist by changing the dried fruit, or try another type of chocolate.

Makes 4 dozen cookies

2 cups all-purpose flour

2½ sticks unsalted butter, at room temperature

1 cup granulated sugar

1 cup dark brown sugar

2 large eggs

2 teaspoons vanilla

2 cups rolled oats (old-fashioned style)

2 cups bittersweet chocolate chips

2 cups dried cranberries (Craisins)

1 cup slivered almonds, lightly toasted and cooled

1 teaspoon baking soda

½ teaspoon salt

1. Preheat your oven to 350°F. In a large bowl, cream (mix) together the butter, sugar, and brown sugar.

2. Add the eggs, vanilla, salt, and baking soda. Mix just to combine. Mix in the flour and oats; don't combine completely.

3. Add the chocolate chips, cranberries, and almonds and mix. Don't overmix the cookie dough, it will become too soft. Chill the dough for 1 to 2 hours.

4. Using a small ice cream scoop or tablespoon, place balls of dough on a parchment-paper–lined baking sheet.

5. Place sheets in the preheated oven, and bake for 14 to 16 minutes, or until golden. Remove from the oven and cool on baking sheets, or slide the parchment paper off the baking sheets and cool on racks.

6. Allow the pans to cool before repeating with any unused dough.

Note: The cookies can be stored in an airtight container for up to 1 week, or frozen.

Molasses Cookies

When I worked as a clinic nurse we frequently shared treats for birthdays or just because. One day a co-worker, Phyllis, brought these cookies to share. We all went crazy! She told us she grew up on a farm, and these were cookies her mom made. It's a big batch. I make them for the bakery using 70 gram balls of dough rather than walnut sized. The cookies are as popular today as the first time I made them. They freeze well, and are even tasty with a little chill from the freezer.

Makes 3 to 6 dozen depending on the size

2 cups vegetable oil

4 cups sugar

1 cup molasses

4 eggs

8 cups flour

1 teaspoon salt

8 teaspoons baking soda

2 teaspoons each cinnamon, ground cloves, and ground ginger

Granulated sugar for rolling dough

1. Preheat your oven to 350°F.
2. Mix all the ingredients together in a mixer using a paddle attachment or by hand until soft dough forms.
3. Roll into balls about the size of a walnut, and roll in granulated sugar.
4. You can also use an ice cream scoop for a BIG cookie! If you weigh the dough, it will weigh about 70 grams or about 2½ ounces. Roll the balls in granulated sugar and set on cookie sheet lined with parchment. If you're making a larger cookie, flatten the ball of dough slightly with your palm, then sprinkle with more sugar.
5. Bake at 350°F for 12 to 15 minutes.

The cookies will puff up, then flatten out. The cookies will have cracks on the top with slightly golden brown edges. Bake a shorter time for soft cookies or longer for crisper. Makes about 6 dozen cookies, depending on size.

Diamant Sablé (French Diamond Butter Cookies)

This is one of the first recipes we made in pastry school. The name of the cookie is diamond because the cookie when rolled in coarse sugar appears to have been rolled in diamonds. They make wonderful party or wedding favors. I like to add a bit of lemon zest to the vanilla version and some cinnamon and cocoa powder to make a chocolate version.

Makes about 3 dozen cookies

2 sticks (225 grams) butter, chilled

2¼ cups (320 grams) all purpose flour

¾ cup (100 grams) confectioners' sugar

½ teaspoon vanilla extract

½ egg (try to get both the white and some yolk)

1 egg white for brushing on the dough

Coarse decorating sugar, white or desired color

Dash of salt

1. On your work surface, cut the butter into the flour. The mixture and bits of butter should be the size of peas.

2. Make a circle with the mixture, with the center open (a well). Add the egg, sugar, salt, and vanilla to the center and mix together with your fingertips. Cut the mixture into the flour and butter.

3. Line the dough in front of you. Using the heel of your hand, smear the dough away from you to shear the dough against the countertop to combine. Gather the dough, and repeat. The dough should be combined after two to three passes. Work quickly so you don't heat and soften the butter.

4. Roll the dough into two logs, about 1 inch in diameter. Wrap each log in parchment or plastic wrap and chill for at least 1 hour.

5. Turn the logs every 15 minutes so the bottom does not get flat. If you have a rounded loaf pan, you can rest the dough on the pan so it will stay in a round shape. Or, place in a paper towel roll.

6. When the dough is well chilled, preheat your oven to 350°F. Unwrap the dough.

7. Place a piece of parchment paper on your work surface, or use a large plate. Make a line of sugar the length of the dough, about ¼ to ½ inch deep and 2 to 3 inches wide. Brush the log with a thin layer of egg white, then roll into the sugar, pressing to adhere the sugar to the logs. Repeat with second log. If the dough feels soft, place in refrigerator for 5 minutes.

8. Slice the dough into ½- to ¾-inch inch slices and place about 1 inch apart on a parchment-lined baking sheet. Reshape as necessary so the cookies are round.

9. Bake 8 to 10 minutes until the cookies are just beginning to brown. Remove from oven and cool. Store in an airtight container for up to 1 week, or freeze.

KITCHEN SINK COOKIES

Here it is! The first cookie I ever made. It's the recipe my mom made and froze in coffee cans in our freezer. When we made cookies in our house, we put all the ingredients in a large bowl and squished the dough with our fingers. When the dough came together, it was ready to shape into balls. If you're using an electric mixer, don't overwork the dough, and be sure to always use the paddle attachment. Use your hands to mix all the ingredients together. Have fun adding or subtracting any of the add-ins you like. Make them your own!

Makes 1 to 2 dozen cookies depending on size

1 cup plus 1 tablespoon shortening

2 eggs

1 cup brown sugar

1 cup granulated sugar

½ teaspoon salt

1 teaspoon baking soda

3 cups old-fashioned oatmeal

1 teaspoon vanilla

Coconut, chocolate chips, wheat germ (any or all, optional)

1. Preheat your oven to 350°F.

2. In a large bowl, cream together the shortening and sugars.

3. Add the eggs and dry ingredients.

4. Add coconut, chocolate chips, or other add-ins.

5. Mix just to combine.

6. Drop by shaggy tablespoons onto a parchment-paper-lined baking sheet.

7. Bake 10 to 12 minutes until slightly golden on the edges.

8. Remove to a cooling rack.

Rolled Sugar Cookies

Everyone I know has a favorite style of rolled cut-out cookie. Some like them them thick, others like them thin. Some like creamy icing, others like glaze. This is the Christmas cookie our family has made for years. The sour cream and nutmeg add a wonderful scent and flavor to the cookies. When I was old enough to roll the dough, the trick was to roll it so thin you could almost see through it. The thin cookies are iced with a simple powdered sugar glaze, then topped with sprinkles.

Makes 4 to 6 dozen depending on the cookie-cutter size

Sugar Cookies:

2 cups all-purpose flour

½ teaspoon baking soda

¼ teaspoon ground nutmeg

¼ teaspoon salt

½ cup unsalted butter (1 stick), room temperature

¾ cup sugar

½ cup sour cream

Icing:

2 cups powdered sugar

⅓ cup milk or water

½ teaspoon vanilla

Sugar Cookies:

1. In a large bowl, whisk together the dry ingredients.

2. In another small bowl cream together the sugar and butter.

3. Add the sour cream.

4. Stir the sour cream mixture into the dry ingredients until the dough comes together.

5. Shape the dough into a ½ inch thick flat disk. Wrap in plastic wrap or parchment paper and chill for at least 1 hour.

6. On a lightly floured surface, roll the dough very thin. If you have a pastry cloth, it will come in handy with this recipe. Be sure the dough is able to move on the work surface by sliding after a few rolls. Dust under the dough as necessary. Cut into desired shapes with cookie cutter.

7. Using a spatula or butter knife, lift the dough and place on a parchment-lined baking sheet.

8. Bake 6 to 8 minutes, until the edges of the cookies are light brown.

9. Remove from the oven, and transfer cookies with a spatula to a wire rack to cool completely.

Icing:

Mix well, and ice cookies with a butter knife or spatula. Sprinkle with colored sugars and sprinkles.

TOFFEE BARS

A cousin to shortbread, these are a family favorite. It wouldn't be Christmas without Toffee Bars. Each year my job was to make this recipe. It's very forgiving, and fun for kids.

Makes one 13x9 inch pan

1 cup dark brown sugar

1 cup (2 sticks) unsalted butter, softened

1 egg

1 teaspoon vanilla extract

2 cups all-purpose flour

¼ teaspoon salt

½ pound chocolate chips (semi-sweet or dark)

½ cup finely chopped walnuts

1. Preheat your oven to 350°F.

2. Grease a 13x9 inch baking pan.

3. Cream together the butter and sugar, and add the egg, vanilla, and salt. Mix together. Mix in the flour.

4. Press the dough into the pan with your fingers.

5. Bake for 20 minutes, until the bars are golden brown.

6. While still hot, sprinkle with the chocolate chips. When the chips have melted, spread across the baked bars, and top with the chopped nuts.

7. When cool, cut into 2x2 inch squares.

PECAN CRESCENTS

I've been baking at the holidays since I can remember. As we got older, our baking jobs changed. One of my first jobs was shaping the crescents. Make a double batch—these will go fast!

Makes about 3 dozen

1 cup shortening
1 cup powdered sugar
½ teaspoon salt
1¼ cups pecans, chopped
2 cups all-purpose flour
1 tablespoon water
1 tablespoon vanilla extract
Powdered sugar for rolling the warm cookies

1. Preheat your oven to 325°F.

2. Mix the ingredients together to form a dough.

3. Pinch off a walnut-sized piece of dough. Roll between your palms to make a log shape about 2 to 2½ inches in length.

4. Place on the parchment-lined baking sheet. Bend the log to form a crescent shape.

5. Bake 12 to 15 minutes, until barely golden brown.

6. When cool enough to handle, roll in powdered sugar.

Raspberry Coconut Bars

My dear friend Kim gave me this recipe years ago. She adds the bars to dessert buffets with her famous wedding cakes. I've been teaching the recipe in all my Summer Picnic classes. The bars are easy, very tasty, and portable. The recipe can be doubled for a jelly roll or half sheet pan.

Makes one 13x9 inch pan

1½ cups sweetened shredded coconut

1¼ cups all-purpose flour

¾ cup brown sugar

¼ cup granulated sugar

½ teaspoon salt

1½ stick unsalted butter, chilled

1½ cups rolled oats (old-fashioned style)

¾ cup good quality raspberry preserves

Shortening or cooking spray for preparing the pan

1. Preheat your oven to 350°F.

2. Place ¾ cup coconut in a thin layer on a baking sheet. Place in oven to toast. Stir every 3 to 4 minutes as the coconut brown. Watch carefully! The coconut can burn very quickly. Remove from the oven and set aside to cool.

3. Brush your pan with shortening or spray with cooking spray.

4. In a food processor, pulse to combine the flour, sugars, salt, and butter. Or mix by hand or with a stand mixer fitted with the paddle attachment. The mixture should be crumbles with pea-sized bits.

5. Add the oats and toasted coconut. Reserve 1 cup of the dough.

6. Press the remaining dough into the pan.

7. Spread the preserves on top of the dough, then crumble the reserved dough over the top.

8. Sprinkle the untoasted coconut on top.

9. Place in the oven and bake for 20 to 25 minutes.

10. Remove from the oven, cool, cut into squares. Store the bars in a cool place in an airtight container for up to 1 week, or freeze.

chapter seven

CAKES

PERFECT BIRTHDAY CHOCOLATE CAKE

This chocolate cake is by far the most popular selling cake at The Little French Bakery for weddings and special occasions. I think it's the perfect birthday cake. It's inspired by the famous recipe on the Hershey cocoa can. Yes, that's true. I've made some adjustments to make the flavors a bit more grownup. I like cakes extra tall so this one uses three 8-inch cake pans. Feel free to make two 12-inch layers instead.

1–2 batches French Buttercream (p. 102)
1–2 batches Chocolate Glaze (p. 150)

For the cake:

4 cups granulated sugar (767 gm)

3½ cups all-purpose flour (348 gm)

1½ cup cocoa powder (167 gm)

1 tablespoon baking powder (11 gm)

1 tablespoon baking soda (13 gm)

2 teaspoons salt (10 gm)

4 large eggs

2 cups low-fat milk

1 cup vegetable oil

1½ cups very warm water

½ cup hot brewed coffee

1½ tablespoons vanilla extract

Butter or vegetable shortening for preparing pans

2–3 tablespoons flour for dusting pans

1. Preheat your oven to 350°F.

2. Using a pastry brush or paper towel brush/wipe pans with shortening. Place flour in the first pan, tap to distribute the flour in a thin layer, then tap into the next pan, and the next. Discard extra flour. Line the pans with circles of parchment paper.

3. Combine the sugar, flour, cocoa, baking powder, soda, and salt in a large mixing bowl or the bowl of a stand mixer fitted with the paddle attachment. Slowly beat the dry ingredients for a few seconds to lighten and combine.

4. Add the oil and vanilla and beat just to combine, 15 seconds at the most. Add the eggs and milk and beat for 1 minute at low speed, then increase speed and beat at medium for 1 more minute. Remove the bowl from the mixer, and fold in the warm water and coffee. Scrape the sides and bottom of the bowl well. The cake batter will be very loose.

5. Place the pans in your oven and bake for 25 to 35 minutes, or until the tops spring back under light pressure, the cakes have pulled away slightly from the edges of the pans, and a toothpick or cake tester inserted into the center comes out clean.

6. Transfer from the oven to a wire rack. Cool completely. When ready to frost, run a dinner knife around the inside of the pan, then turn over and tap out the cake. Be sure to remove the parchment circles before icing.

To assemble: Using a cardboard circle, place the first cake top side against the cardboard. Fill with ⅓-½ inch frosting. Place the next cake, top side against the frosting, add a layer of frosting. Place the final layer, bottom side up. Finish frosting the cake by making pretty peaks with the icing or use a spatula to create a smooth surface. Using a spatula, transfer the cake to the serving platter, or a larger cake board covered with a pretty paper doily.

Chocolate Glaze and Filling

To make a cake even more special, adding glaze will take it over the top. When the glaze is warm, it can be poured onto the top of the cake. You'll want to pipe a border to keep the glaze from running over the edges. When the glaze cools to room temperature, it can be spread and used as a filling between the layers of cake. The corn syrup makes the glaze shiny. The water keeps it shiny when it's chilled. You may wish to make one batch to fill the cake and a second to pour over the cake. Dip strawberries, apricots, and bananas with any leftover glaze.

1⅓ cups (240 grams) semi-sweet or bittersweet chocolate

12 tablespoons or 1½ sticks (180 grams) unsalted butter

1 tablespoon light corn syrup (non-high-fructose)

5 teaspoons warm water

1. Place all ingredients in a microwave bowl. Heat for 1 minute, remove, and stir to melt the chocolate and emulsify the butter into the mixture. Repeat until the glaze is smooth. Though glaze will be warm, it may need to rest a few minutes to melt the tiny bits of chips. If you use couverture or fine bar chocolate, the chocolate will be smoother.

2. Let the glaze cool slightly and pour onto the cake. Or cover and allow to rest at room temperature. When firm, spoon into the piping bag or use a spatula to spread as you would icing. The firm glaze can also be transferred into a piping bag fitted with a large decorative tip and piped to create a cake border.

Pumpkin Loaves and Cupcakes

I'm not a huge fan of carrot cakes loaded with fresh grated carrot. This recipe brings all the flavor of a carrot cake, but with pumpkin. Add in all the favorite extras, and you've got a great cake. Not a coconut fan? It's fine to leave it out. Just increase the flour by ¼ cup, and garnish the cake with chopped walnuts instead of coconut.

Makes one 8-inch two-layer cake

3 cups sugar

1½ cups vegetable oil

1 tablespoon cinnamon

1 tablespoon baking soda

1 tablespoon vanilla extract

1 teaspoon salt

4 whole eggs

3¼ cups all-purpose flour

1 15-ounce can pumpkin puree (pureed canned carrots work great too!)

1 cup grated (canned) pineapple, drained

1½ cup chopped walnuts

3 cups shredded flaked coconut, divided

1. Preheat your oven to 350°F. Prepare your pans. You could make 12 cupcakes plus four 4x6 paper mold loaves, or two 9-inch layer cakes. If using cake pans, begin by brushing/wiping with shortening then dusting with flour. Line the pans with parchment paper.

2. In a large bowl combine the sugar, oil, cinnamon, sugar, salt, eggs, and flour. Using a mixer, mix until combined, about 2 minutes. Mix in the pumpkin, pineapple, 1 cup of coconut, and the walnuts. If you are using carrots, puree them until smooth in a food processor.

3. Spread batter into the pans. Fill the cupcakes ⅔ full. An ice cream scoop will work great for scooping the dough into the cups. Fill the loaf and cake pans about two thirds full. Tap pans to remove any bubbles.

4. Bake the cupcakes 12 to 15 minutes, and the cakes 25 to 35 minutes or until golden brown, the top springs back, and a toothpick inserted into the center comes out clean without wet batter.

5. Cool the cakes on a wire rack. When completely cool, frost the cake with Cream Cheese Icing in big sweeping peaks, and top with toasted coconut or chopped nuts.

TIP! To toast the coconut, spread evenly on a baking sheet. Bake at 350°F for 4 to 6 minutes, watching carefully. Remove the pan from the oven and with a spatula, turn the coconut to help brown on all sides. Place pan back in the oven and continue baking 4 to 6 more minutes, until most of the coconut is golden brown.

Confetti Angel Food Cake

While some prefer layer cakes, this is my birthday cake of choice. It's complete with the pink fluffy icing.

Makes one Angel Food Cake

1¾ cups sugar (process 2 minutes in food processor to make super fine)

¼ teaspoon salt

1 cup cake flour, sifted twice

12 egg whites (not a speck of yolk!)

⅓ cup warm water

1 teaspoon vanilla extract

1½ teaspoons cream of tartar

2–3 tablespoons multicolored sprinkles or Jimmies

1. Preheat your oven to 350°F.

2. In a food processor process the sugar about 2 minutes until it is superfine. Mix half of the sugar with the salt and cake flour, setting the remaining sugar aside.

3. Place egg whites in a bowl; set that bowl over another bowl filled with warm water. Gently swish the egg whites until they feel slightly warmer than room temperature. The eggs will whip better and you won't need to wait hours for the eggs to warm at room temperature. When you are ready to proceed, combine egg whites, water, vanilla extract, and cream of tartar in the bowl of your mixer. Using a hand mixer or stand mixer, whip the egg mixture until foamy. Slowly sift the remaining sugar into the egg whites, raise the mixer speed to medium/high. Continue until medium peaks form. The egg whites should make peaks that may droop slightly after a few moments.

4. Sprinkle some of the flour mixture to dust the top of the egg mixture. Using a spatula fold in very gently. Fold in the remaining flour mixture with sprinkles in two to three parts, gently folding well each time.

5. Carefully spoon mixture into an ungreased angel food cake pan. Bake for 35 minutes then test for doneness with a wooden skewer or toothpick. (The skewer should come out clean and dry).

6. Cool upside down on cooling rack for at least an hour before removing from pan. My mom always propped the pan upside down on top of a bottle.

FLUFFY ANGEL FOOD CAKE FROSTING

This is the best icing for an angel food cake. Don't let the one egg fool you. You'll have plenty of icing.

1 egg white
1 cup sugar
½ teaspoon vanilla
¼ teaspoon cream of tartar
½ cup boiling water
1–2 drops food coloring (red or pink will make pink)

1. Mix all the ingredients *except* boiling water in large mixing bowl.
2. Add boiling water all at once and beat 5 to 7 minutes on high until light, fluffy, and a good spreading consistency.
3. Don't overbeat or the mixture will become grainy.

> **TIP!** To fold in the flour, hold the spatula so that the narrow edge is touching the batter. Gently cut straight down the center into the batter. From the bottom turn the spatula and bring it up the side of the bowl, while turning the bowl. Lift the batter on the spatula up and onto the top of the mixture. Take your time, and repeat this step until the mixture is combined. With this technique you won't deflate the egg whites you've worked so hard to create.

Marry Me Flourless Chocolate Cake

I first made this cake for Gary in 1987. My roommate and I were having a holiday party and invited Gary and his daughter, Stephanie, to join the fun. I had heard through the grapevine it was also going to be his birthday. Everyone needs a birthday cake, so I made this one. Midway through the evening I snuck up to the loft with a friend, lit the candles, and walked down the stairs with the cake. We weren't *really* even dating yet, but I think this may have helped fan the flame.

The cake is dense, rich, and very chocolatey. I've found it appeals to those who claim not to really like chocolate. You can serve it at room temperature or cold. Invite friends because one cake goes a very long way. Use any bittersweet/semisweet you like. Just not milk chocolate, it will be too sweet. I've adapted this recipe from *The Silver Palate Cookbook* by Sheila Lukins and Julie Rosso to be gluten free.

Makes 20 servings (small . . . but rich)

14 ounces semisweet chocolate (the darker, the better)

12 eggs, separated

2 cups granulated sugar

3½ sticks butter, softened

1 cup unbleached all-purpose flour, sifted (or 1 cup of Cup4Cup gluten-free flour)

Confectioners' sugar for serving

1. Preheat your oven to 325°F. Butter and sugar a 10-inch springform pan. Tap out any excess sugar.

2. Break or chop the chocolate into small pieces and melt in microwave or in a pan placed over another pan of barely simmering water. Stir until smooth, and cool slightly. Be careful not to burn the chocolate.

3. Beat the egg yolks and sugar until they are pale and light yellow. When you lift the whisk or beater over the mixture, there should be a ribbon of the mixture that falls from the beaters and gently lays on top of the egg/sugar mixture. Add the chocolate and mix thoroughly. Stir in the butter.

4. In another bowl, beat the egg whites until they are stiff. Add a large spoonful of the chocolate mixture into the egg whites and fold gently. Then add the egg whites to the chocolate mixture, folding very gently until mixed. Be very careful not to overmix and deflate the batter.

5. Pour the batter into the prepared pan (it will come close to the top) and set on the middle rack and bake for 1 hour and 20 minutes. A cake tester or toothpick should come out clean when inserted into the center of the cake. The cake will rise and crack, but will settle as it cools. Cool on a rack for 15 to 20 minutes, then release the ring of the springform pan. Allow the cake to cool, then refrigerate until cold. It's best to wait until the cake is cold to remove the bottom of the springform.

6. To serve sift with powdered (confectioners') sugar, and some whipped cream, if desired. To make it extra special, set a doily on the cake and sift the powdered sugar on the top, then gently lift off the doily.

Banana Cake with Cream Cheese Icing

One of my customers asked me to make a banana cake for a family event. The recipe made a very small batch. I've adapted the original recipe for larger cakes and cupcakes. The cream cheese icing adds the finishing touch. Top with chopped walnuts or toasted coconut.

3 sticks (1½ cups) unsalted butter

3¾ cups (719 grams) sugar

6 large eggs

1 tablespoon (13 grams) baking soda

¾ cup sour cream

3 cups mashed, ripe bananas

4½ cups (405 grams) cake flour, sifted

1 teaspoon (5 grams) salt

1 tablespoon vanilla extract

1. Preheat your oven to 350°F. Grease and flour three 8-inch round baking pans. Line with parchment and set aside.

2. In a mixing bowl, or the bowl of a stand mixer fitted with a paddle attachment, cream sugar and butter together. Add the extract, salt, and baking soda, and mix well.

3. Add the eggs, beating after each addition.

4. Add the flour alternating with the sour cream. Mix well. Fold in the bananas.

5. Divide the batter between the prepared pans.

6. Place in the oven and bake 20 to 25 minutes or until a toothpick inserted into the center comes out clean and the cake springs back to light touch.

7. Cool completely, then frost.

ORANGE CARAMEL LAYER CAKE

This pretty cake is wonderful any time of the year. It's perfect for a garden wedding. The citrus flavor adds a burst of spring, while the caramel brings the warmth of autumn.

For the cake:

²/₃ cup milk (1 or 2 percent or whole)

6 tablespoons unsalted butter

1 teaspoon vanilla extract

2 teaspoons orange extract

2²/₃ cups (239 grams) cake flour

1½ teaspoon (6 grams) baking powder

½ teaspoon (2.5 grams) salt

6 large eggs

²/₃ cup (127 grams) sugar

Juice of one orange (about ⅓ cup)

For the caramel:

1 cup (192 grams) granulated sugar

½ cup water

1¼ cup orange juice

Zest of one orange, about 1 tablespoon

1 tablespoon butter, softened

1 teaspoon cornstarch

Shortening or soft butter and flour for preparing pans

1. Preheat your oven to 350°F. Using three 6- or two 8-inch cake pans, brush each pan with shortening or softened butter. Dust with a generous layer of flour, and line the bottom with parchment paper. Set aside.

2. Using a mixer, place the butter, sugar, and vanilla in the bowl and beat until very light and fluffy.

3. Mix in the baking powder and salt.

4. Beat in the eggs one at a time, beating well after each addition. Starting with the flour, add one third of the flour, mix well. Add one half of the milk and beat to combine. Repeat with one-third flour, one-half milk, and finish with the final third of the flour. Scrape the bowl frequently and as needed.

5. Divide the batter between the cake pans. Place in the oven and bake for 25 to 30 minutes or until a cake tester or toothpick inserted into the center comes out clean, and the cake has pulled away slightly from the edge of the pan.

6. Remove pans to a wire rack and cool completely.

While the cakes are baking make the caramel:

1. In a large saucepan, add the water, then the sugar. Heat over medium heat until the mixture becomes a deep amber color. Do not stir as this will cause the mixture to crystalize.

2. In another small pan, heat the orange juice with the zest to a simmer. When the caramel is ready, lower the heat and pour the orange juice into the caramel. Be very careful, the mixture will spit, bubble, and boil very hard. As the bubbling subsides, stir to pick up any caramel on the bottom and to dissolve any small pieces of caramel.

3. Simmer for 4 to 5 minutes to reduce slightly.

4. Strain into a heat-proof small bowl or measuring cup and cool. This is the imbibing syrup. Reserve ½ cup.

For the icing caramel:

1. Return the reserved cup of syrup to the saucepan.

2. Add the cornstarch, whisk, and bring to a boil. Remove from the heat.

3. Allow the caramel to cool slightly, then stir in the butter. Allow the mixture to cool. The caramel will have thickened. When cool, fold to your taste into the cream cheese icing.

To assemble your cake:

1. Turn the cake pans upside down and rap against the work surface. The cakes will drop from the pans.

2. Place the first cake bottom-side up on a cake board.

3. With a pastry brush, brush generously with the imbibing syrup. Spread a layer of icing on the cake and add the next layer.

4. Imbibe, and add another layer of icing. Finish with the last layer. Imbibe. Spread the cake with the remaining icing in pretty peaks. Chill the cake for at least 2 hours.

5. Garnish with fresh fruits or food-safe fresh flowers.

CREAM CHEESE ICING

3–8 packages cream cheese, at room temperature

½ stick unsalted butter, at room temperature

1 cup confectioners' sugar

1 teaspoon vanilla extract

1 pinch salt

1. Beat together the butter and cream cheese.
2. Add the confectioners' sugar and vanilla. If the mixture is too loose to spread, cover and chill. When ready to use, allow the icing to come to just below room temperature before use. It will be much easier to spread.
3. For the Orange Caramel Cake, add cooled caramel to the icing to taste and mix well.

chapter eight

FAVORITE MEALS

Holiday Beef Tenderloin with Horseradish Sauce on Baguettes

Preparing meat dishes was always intimidating to me. First, you had to find the right cut of meat in the grocery or butcher shop. Then, once you got the meat home, there was fat, bone, that shiny silvery stuff connecting the muscle (silverskin). Yes, I know it has a name, but in my mind, it's that shiny, silvery stuff. How long to cook? To brown first or not? And just touching raw meat and chicken gave me the creeps.

Enter beef tenderloin. This beautiful cut of meat is one of the most delicious, and it's easy to prepare for those new to the meat world. The first time I made beef tenderloin it was following the recipe of Ina Garten. Her recipe calls for a 5-pound tenderloin. I've made it for the last several years for holiday dinners. I try to buy the best filet in the case, which means it's about a $100 piece of meat. Divided among many friends, that's not too bad, but it is steep.

Sometimes for cost and quantity reasons, it's nice to use a smaller filet. My favorite way to serve this recipe is on baguettes sliced on a long diagonal, with horseradish sauce. I slice the beef very thin, and serve it warm with crumbled blue cheese and horseradish mixed into mayonnaise. Everyone gathers around the cutting board and makes open-faced sandwiches. There's never a scrap left. Adapted from *The Barefoot Contessa* by Ina Garten.

Serves 4 to 6

For the Tenderloin:

1 (2½–5 pound) fillet of beef

1–2 tablespoons unsalted butter, at room temperature

1 tablespoon sea salt

1 tablespoon freshly ground black pepper

For the Sauce:

4 tablespoons prepared horseradish (not spread or sauce)

1 cup mayonnaise

½ teaspoon freshly ground black pepper

1. Preheat your oven to 500°F.

2. With a sharp thin knife, trim any silverskin from the tenderloin. If the tenderloin has different thicknesses, fold the ends of the filet over to create a uniform thickness and tie with cotton string. This will ensure your meat is cooked consistently throughout. As tenderloins increase in size, they generally remain about the same diameter, but increase in length. I err on the side of having the meat rare. I can always continue cooking, but I can't undo an overcooked piece of meat.

3. Allow the meat to come to room temperature (about 1 hour).

4. Place the tenderloin on a baking sheet pan or in a roasting pan. Pat the outside dry with a paper towel. With your hands, spread the butter over the tenderloin. Sprinkle evenly with the salt and pepper.

5. Place the pan in the oven, and roast for 23 minutes for medium-rare. When you remove the pan from the oven, press the meat with your finger. For medium rare, it should feel like you're pressing on your cheek with your mouth closed, but not as firm as your nose. Cover the beef immediately

with foil and allow the meat to rest for 15 to 20 minutes. This resting time is critical to finish the cooking process. If the tenderloin is smaller, reduce the cooking and resting time by a few minutes.

6. Uncover the filet, remove the strings, and with a sharp knife, slice into very thin slices. Serve with baguette slices with crumbled blue cheese, caramelized onions, and horseradish on the side.

BOEUF BOURGUIGNON

When I think of a classic French meal, I think of this recipe. It's one of the most satisfying, comforting dishes I've ever made. The smells from the kitchen are incredible. If you've got time for the long simmer, you're all set. Serve this wonderful meal with lots of crusty bread, and a salad for a fancy or casual meal. I've always deferred to Julia Child's version with a few modifications. Take your time, and savor every step.

Serves 4 to 6

For the Stew:

6 strips bacon, thick cut if possible

1 tablespoon olive oil

1 beef shoulder or blade roast, about 4 pounds

2 carrots, peeled and sliced into ¼-inch slices (coins)

1 large onion, peeled and coarsely chopped

1 teaspoon salt

1 teaspoon black pepper

2–3 tablespoons all-purpose flour

1 bottle red wine (Bordeaux, Burgundy, or Chianti)

2–3 cups low-salt beef stock, fat skimmed

1 tablespoon tomato paste

2–3 cloves garlic, minced

2–3 sprigs fresh thyme, or 1 teaspoon minced

1 bay leaf

For the Onions:

1 bag frozen white pearl onions, thawed and drained

1 tablespoon unsalted butter

1 tablespoon olive oil

½ cup beef stock

Salt and pepper

For the Mushrooms:

1 pound button mushrooms, brushed clean and quartered

2 tablespoons unsalted butter

1 tablespoon olive oil

1. Trim any silverskin and large pieces of fat from the roast. Cube the meat into 1½–2 inch cubes. Using a kitchen towel, or paper towel, dry each piece of meat. Set aside.

2. For the stew, slice the bacon crosswise into ¼–⅓-inch wide strips. Place the bacon pieces in a saucepan filled with water. Bring to a boil and simmer for 10 minutes. This will remove much of the fat and the smoky flavor. Drain the bacon, and place on a plate lined with a paper towel. Pat dry.

3. Preheat your oven to 450°F.

4. In a large cast enamel casserole with a lid, heat 1 tablespoon of olive oil over medium heat. Add the bacon and cook 2 to 3 minutes until the bacon is browned. Using a slotted spoon or spatula, carefully remove the bacon from the pan.

5. At this point, you can drain the fat from the pan (keep the brown bits in the bottom of the pan) and add new oil, or add the cubes of beef to the bacon fat/oil. Be sure the oil is hot.

6. Add the meat in one layer. Don't try to move the meat for a few minutes. If the meat is ready to be turned, it will lift easily; if not, it will tear. Turn the cubes so they brown on all sides. Remove them

> **TIP!** Yes, you really do need to dry off each piece of meat. It will help with the browning, and make the final dish much better. Don't buy too fancy of a cut of meat. The meat will be very tender after simmering. A fine cut of meat will deteriorate too much and disappear into the sauce. Spoken from experience!

from the casserole and place on the plate with the bacon. Continue browning all the meat, adding more oil as needed.

7. When all the meat is browned, add the carrots and onion. Cook over medium heat until the onions are translucent. Drain any extra fat.

8. Add the bacon and beef back into the pan. Sprinkle the salt, pepper, and flour over the meat and vegetables, and toss to coat with flour.

9. Place the pan, uncovered, in the oven and heat for 4 to 5 minutes. Remove the pan from the oven, quickly stir to redistribute the ingredients, and place back in the oven for another 5 minutes.

10. Remove the pan from the oven. Reduce the oven temperature to 325°F.

11. Add 3 cups of wine (and pour one for yourself!) and stock to the casserole. The meat should just be covered. Add the tomato paste, garlic, bay leaf, and thyme.

12. Bring the mixture to a low boil over medium heat, and then reduce to a simmer. Place the cover on the casserole, and then place in the oven.

13. Adjust the heat after 5 to 10 minutes, so the liquid is simmering. Continue cooking for 3 to 4 hours. The meat should be fork tender.

14. In the last hour begin preparing the onion and mushroom.

For the onions:

Heat the butter and oil over medium heat. Add the onions and roll in the pan to cook slowly. Try not to brown too quickly. Add the stock. Continue rolling the onions and cook until the stock has reduced to a thick glaze and the onion are tender and glistening. Set aside.

For the mushrooms:

Melt the butter and oil over medium heat. Add the mushroom and gently sauté until the liquid releases from the mushroom then evaporates. Set aside.

Remove the bay leaf and any thyme sprigs from the casserole. Add the onions and mushrooms. Stir gently to combine.

Serve from the casserole or transfer to plates or a large serving platter with sides. Potatoes, noodles, or crusty bread are wonderful accompaniments.

Oven-Roasted Brussels Sprouts and Cauliflower

A few years ago I tried roasting Brussels sprouts for an autumn dinner party. Even our friends who claim not to like Brussels sprouts loved them prepared this way. The best part is they require very little attention and can roast in the thin baking sheet while the rest of your meal is cooking. Cauliflower and fennel can be prepared exactly the same way. Try mixing them together for an autumn dinner.

2–3 pounds fresh Brussels sprouts

2–3 tablespoons olive oil

Salt and black pepper

1. Preheat your oven to 375–400°F.

2. Wash and pat dry the Brussels sprouts.

3. With the paring knife, trim the stem off each sprout, then make an X cut in the bottom. It doesn't need to be more than ⅛-¼ inch deep.

4. Place all the sprouts on the baking sheet.

5. Sprinkle with the olive oil and toss to coat the vegetables. Sprinkle with salt and pepper.

6. Cover with the parchment paper, then cover and seal with the foil.

7. Place in the pan in the oven. It's fine to put it on a shelf below another where other food is cooking. Just not too close to the bottom, especially in an electric oven.

8. Roast for 30 minutes. Carefully open the edge of foil taking care to avoid the hot steam that will escape. With the spatula, toss the vegetables and reseal. Reduce the oven to 350°F and roast for an additional 30 minutes. If your oven is set for another recipe, roast at that temperature. If it's cooler, the vegetables will take longer to roast.

9. The vegetables should be very tender, and caramelized. Remove from the roasting pan to a serving bowl. Add a sprinkle of sea salt for garnish.

CATERING CHICKEN

This mouth-watering dish is a wonderful dish for large crowds. I've adapted the recipe from *The Silver Palate Cookbook* by Sheila Lukins and Julie Rosso.

2–3 chickens, cut into eight or four pieces

1 head of garlic, peeled and finely chopped

¼ cup dried oregano

1 teaspoon ground black pepper

½ teaspoon salt

½ cup red wine vinegar

½ cup olive oil

1 cup pitted prunes

½ cup pitted Spanish green olives (with or without pimentos)

½ cup capers with juice

6 bay leaves

1 cup brown sugar

1 cup white wine

¼ cup Italian parsley or flat leaf parsley, finely chopped

1. In a large bowl or baking dish, combine chicken quarters, garlic, oregano, pepper, salt to taste, vinegar, olive oil, prunes, olives, capers with their juice, and bay leaves.

2. Cover and refrigerate overnight.

3. To finish, preheat your oven to 350°F.

4. Arrange chicken in single layer on one or two large baking dishes or foil roasting pans.

5. Spoon marinade over the chicken. Be sure to include the capers, olives, and prunes. Sprinkle the brown sugar over the chicken, and then gently pour white wine on top.

6. Bake for 50 minutes to 1 hour, until the chicken is cooked through and juices run clear.

7. Using a spoon or baster, check the chicken about every 15 minutes, and baste with pan liquids. I like to serve the chicken family style with the prunes, capers, and a sprinkle of parsley on top. The chicken pairs well with rice, couscous, or oven-roasted potatoes.

YES, YOU TOO CAN MAKE RIBS

Ribs are a summer favorite of mine, yet were always a mystery. Why would there be competitions and rib joints everywhere if they're something you can make at home? This recipe requires very little time with the ribs. Let them go 2½ hours for very tender ribs or reduce the time to 1½ to 2 hours for a rib you can nibble on. I love the combination of the oven and the grill. The ribs are completely cooked when they go on the grill. The grill will add flavor and turn the BBQ sauce into a thick glaze for your ribs.

2 racks baby pork ribs

3 large onions, thinly sliced

1 teaspoon garlic powder

1 bottle dark beer (or whatever you have on hand)

½ cup brewed coffee

Salt/pepper

1 recipe Cowgirl BBQ Sauce, divided for basting and for serving

1. Preheat your oven to 325°F.

2. On a large baking sheet with sides (a jelly roll pan), pile and spread the onions. Place the ribs on the pan. Sprinkle with garlic powder, salt, and pepper.

3. Pour the beer and coffee over the ribs. Seal the pans tightly with foil, and place in the oven.

4. After 2 hours, check the ribs. If they feel nearly tender, remove from the oven. You'll need to time this with lighting your grill. If you're using a gas grill, it's a bit easier to have your grill ready. Transfer the ribs to a large platter.

5. When your grill is hot, transfer the ribs to a medium heat area on the grill.

6. Baste with BBQ sauce, heat for 3 to 5 minutes, turn, and repeat. Serve the ribs immediately with extra sauce.

Cowgirl BBQ Sauce

1 cup ketchup

2 tablespoons soy sauce

2 tablespoons apple cider vinegar

3 tablespoons brown sugar

3 tablespoons tomato paste

2 teaspoons Worcestershire sauce

1 small onion, finely minced

2 cloves garlic, finely minced

½ cup water

1 teaspoon garlic powder

½ teaspoon salt

1 teaspoon ground black pepper

1 tablespoon olive oil

1. In a saucepan, add the olive oil. Heat over medium heat until warm. Add the onions and cook until they are translucent, above 5 minutes. Add the minced garlic and cook another 1 to 2 minutes.

2. Add the remaining ingredients and cook for 20 minutes. Adjust salt and pepper. Use immediately for ribs, or cool, cover, and store in refrigerator. Keeps 2 to 3 days.

chapter nine

SOUPS

story: your first night in paris

It's so hard to explain to someone the feeling of being in Paris. There are so many amazing cities, yet Paris gets into your heart and never leaves. Every time I get back to Paris it's like seeing a dear friend. Make that an old flame who gives you butterflies in your stomach and that sweet crush feeling. People write or call me to tell me they're going to Paris and wonder if I have any suggestions. Do I? You bet. I've kept lists of Paris's places and people over the years. I've got directions and how-tos for finding copper pans and other cooking supplies. I can help you with the best time to see the Eiffel Tower, and offer other suggestions for shopping and eating.

The first and most important advice I can give is to get out and immerse yourself in Paris. Meet her, and let the romance begin. For most of my friends, the flight is about seven hours. The plane lands in the morning. It's exciting, yet your body is wondering when do we eat? Can we sleep? My stomach always feels a little queasy after the flight. I'm not sure if it's excitement or the hangover feeling of jet lag. After finding a taxi and getting to the hotel it's mid-morning to lunch time. Call me crazy, but my advice for jet lag is eat and walk. Best food? Eat protein. Have an omelette and walk. Not fast, just walk. Take it all in. The sights, the smells, the sounds. Take it easy, nap if you must, but not too long. The best part of the day awaits. As the sun is setting, find your way to the Metro. Exit at the stop Pont Marie.

If you haven't ventured far from your hotel yet, you'll pop up out of the Metro and get your first view of the Seine. The City of Light awaits you. It doesn't matter if it's a perfect summer evening, or a drizzling, cold winter night. Suddenly, nothing seems to matter. Walk across the Pont Marie and take time to look up and down the river. Barges, lovers, beautiful buildings, and the Eiffel Tower twinkling in the distance. You're crossing the bridge to Ille St. Louis, the smaller of the two islands in the middle of the Seine River in Paris. I've always wondered who lives in the beautiful apartments lining the streets. What must it be like to live there? What if I did? Of course I'd have to be wearing pretty red velvet shoes! Now just ahead on rue St-Louis-en-l'Ile is a very special restaurant, L'ilot Vache. My first trip to this gem was in 1998. Since then, I visit every time I'm there. This is also where I celebrated a very big "zero" birthday. When you walk in, the aromas and decor envelope you. The old beams, centuries old, must have hours of stories they could tell. There are flowers stretching to the ceiling in huge vases making a canopy over the tables. Guests laugh and chatter. This is my Paris.

I had never had *soupe de poisson* before. If it wasn't for my friend, Kim, insisting I try it, I still may not have had it. My first thought was why would I eat fish soup when there are other beautiful items on the menu. It's not just soup, it's the experience. Here's how it works. I call it The Show. The waiter brings warm bowls and distributes them along with platters of small bowls containing rouille (spicy mayonnaise), grated gruyere cheese, and croutons. He disappears and returns with a large soup tureen. Each person passes their bowl to be filled with the steaming, piping hot soup. It's smooth, reddish brown in color, opaque, rich. You pick up a crouton, dip it in the rouille, then the gruyere, and drop the crouton of goodness into the soup. The cheese immediately starts melting, and the rouille blends into the soup. It's warm, welcoming, and the perfect start to your first dinner in Paris.

My Prix Fixe (menu) is always the same. I follow the soup with Salmon with Two Sauces, and Chocolate Mousse. I know I should try other menu items, but it's become ritual. As you leave the restaurant the street lights twinkle, snow may be falling, and you're tired, happy, and full from a spectacular meal. Most of all, you now know why people love Paris. Here's a way to bring back those fond memories, and the love of Paris.

Soupe De Poisson with Rouille and Croûtons

Serves 6 for appetizer course

For the Soup:

2–2½ pounds mixed fish such as cod, haddock, snapper, or sole (I prefer to purchase filets)

⅓ cup olive oil

½ cup chopped onion (1 small-medium)

2 stalks chopped celery

1 leek (very well washed, and white and light green part) chopped

¼–⅓ chopped fennel bulb (about ½ cup)

3 garlic cloves, coarsely chopped

Juice of orange, plus zest

1 14-ounce (small) can, or 2–3 fresh peeled, chopped tomatoes

1 small red pepper, seeds and core removed and coarsely chopped

1 bay leaf

2 sprigs thyme

1 pinch of saffron

¼ pound peeled, cooked shrimp with tails removed

1 pinch of cayenne pepper

4–6 cups good quality fish/seafood stock

1 tablespoon Pernod liqueur (optional)

For the Croûtons:

1 baguette, cut into ½–¾ inch cubes

Olive oil

Salt and pepper

For the Rouille (pronounced roo-ee)

3 egg yolks (see tip box)

1 teaspoon Dijon mustard

4 garlic cloves, chopped

1 tablespoon of white wine

½ teaspoon of cayenne pepper

1½ cups of olive oil

1 tablespoon lemon juice

Salt

Rouille:

1. Place the egg yolks, mustard, and garlic in a food processor and blend all the ingredients for 30 seconds to make a purée. With the motor running, slowly drizzle in the olive oil until the mixture is smooth. It will be thick. Pulse in the wine.

2. Transfer to a small bowl. Adjust the seasonings with salt and lemon juice. Stir in the cayenne pepper to taste. The rouille should be spicy. Store in refrigerator.

Soup:

1. Slice the filets into 2-inch chunks, remove any bones. In a stock pot or large pan, heat the olive oil. Add the vegetables, and cook over medium heat until the onions are translucent, about 5 minutes. Don't allow the vegetables to brown too much.

2. Add the orange zest, tomatoes, red pepper, bay leaf, thyme, saffron, shrimp, cayenne pepper, and fish. Cook for 2 to 3 minutes, then add 5 cups of stock and orange juice, bring to a boil, then reduce the heat to a simmer.

3. Simmer the soup for 1 hour.

Croûtons:

1. Preheat the oven to 400 °F. Cut the baguette in ½–¾ inch cubes and lay them in a single layer on a baking sheet.

2. Brush or drizzle lightly with olive oil (one side is fine) then sprinkle lightly with salt and pepper.

3. Bake 7 to 10 minutes until crisp but not hard. Watch carefully so they don't toast too dark or burn. Some ovens may only require 5 minutes.

4. Remove from baking sheet to a small basket or bowl.

To Finish:

1. Carefully remove the bay leaf and any stems of thyme.

2. Transfer the soup to a blender. You may need to do this in batches. Be very careful, the soup is hot! Purée the soup. You may wish to pass the soup through a sieve (strainer) into a clean bowl or another pot. Press out as much liquid as possible.

3. Return the soup to the heat and season to taste with the cayenne, salt, and pepper. The soup can be thinned with the remaining seafood stock. Keep the soup very warm.

4. To serve, ladle the piping hot soup into bowls, preferably at the table. Present the rouille, croutons, and grated gruyere in small bowls. Each person will dip croûtons into the rouille, then into the finely grated gruyere, and drop into his or her soup.

the belly of paris

I'm very sentimental about historical treasures and places. I have a treasure to share with you. There's a neighborhood in Paris called Les Halles. Starting in the 1100s, vendors brought carts of their produce and goods to this large market. It was nicknamed "the belly of Paris" by Émile Zola in his novel, *Le Ventre de Paris*. The beautiful St. Eustache cathedral in the midst of the market is one of the oldest cathedrals in Paris and is still open for services today. In 1971, the market was moved to the outskirts of Paris, making room for a city park. Some refer to this as the day the heart of Paris died. There is still a small market with cookware stores still dotting the neighborhood. Inside St. Eustache there is a carved panel paying tribute, showing the merchants with their loaded carts, tears streaming down their cheeks, leaving the market for the last time. It's a very moving work of art. Oh how I wish I could have seen the market in its day, bustling with sights, and smells.

As the story was told to me by one of our pastry school chefs, vendors prepared for customers in the wee hours of the morning cleaning, slicing, sorting, and butchering. For an early breakfast or late night meal they would make a fire, roast some beef bones and onions, then add water to make a soup. After a good simmer, they would add pieces of day-old bread and top it with some scraps of cheese. Yes, you guessed it. Onion Soup Gratinée, or French Onion Soup. With deepest respect for the merchants and the heart of Paris, I offer this recipe.

It's not fast, but it's not difficult. It does require time, and it's well worth it. I promise it will quite possibly be the best you've ever had. A rich, not too salty broth with perfectly caramelized onions topped with a crisp baguette and melted cheese. Adapted from Thomas Keller's Onion Soup, *Bouchon Cookbook*.

SOUPE À L'OIGNON GRATINÉE (ONION SOUP)

For the Caramelized Onions:

8–10 large yellow onions

½ stick unsalted butter

2 tablespoons olive oil

Salt

For the Soup:

1 tablespoon all-purpose flour

3 quarts Beef Stock, low/no salt if using prepared stock

1½–2 cups caramelized onions

Freshly ground black pepper

Sherry or red wine vinegar

Bouquet:

1 piece cheesecloth or 1 outer leek leaf

Kitchen twine

8–10 black peppercorns

1 sprig thyme

1 bay leaf

(Place herbs in cheesecloth and tie with twine. This will allow you to remove easily from the soup)

For the Croutons:

1 baguette

Olive oil

Salt and pepper

Garnish:

Comte or Emmentaler (Swiss) cheese, grated and/or ⅛ inch thick slices

Caramelized Onions:

1. Start with eight to ten large yellow onions, organic if possible. Peel off the skin, then cut off the top and root end. Slice the onion in half top to bottom.

2. Place the onion cut side down on a cutting board. You'll notice lines in the onion running the length of the onion. Slice thin strips using the lines as a guide. This will cut through tiny membranes in the onion and make them break down easier while caramelizing. You'll fill a big stock pot with onion.

3. Melt the butter in a large stockpot or cast enamel pan. Add the olive oil and the onions. Raise the heat and slowly begin cooking the onions. Be very careful not to brown them. Don't add the salt yet. When the onions have wilted, add the salt. The onions will let off a great deal of liquid.

4. Continue stirring and checking about every 10 minutes. The liquid will reduce as the onions cook and caramelize. Continue cooking the onions until they are the color of caramel and nearly as dark as root beer. Dark and creamy. This may take six to eight hours. Take your time, don't rush them.

5. For the soup, you'll need 1½–2 cups of caramelized onions. You can freeze the rest, or make Caramelized Onion Dip.

Soup:

1. In a large stock pot, place the caramelized onions and sprinkle with flour. Cook for a few minutes, then add the beef stock and the bouquet garni.

2. Bring to a boil, then reduce to a simmer. Simmer until the mixture is reduced by half.

184   *The Little French Bakery Cookbook*

3. Remove the bouquet and discard. Add the vinegar and adjust seasonings with salt and pepper.

4. To prepare the croutons, slice baguettes in $1/2$–$3/4$ inch slices. Preheat oven to 400°F. Place oven rack in center position. Arrange slices in a single layer on a baking sheet. Brush with olive oil and sprinkle lightly with salt and pepper.

5. Place in oven and bake until crisp and lightly browned but not hard. This will be about 7 to 10 minutes. Watch carefully!

6. Turn oven to broil. Keep the oven rack in the center of the oven. Place oven-proof ramekins or bowls on a baking sheet lined with parchment or a silicone mat to prevent cheese from sticking and burning.

7. Ladle the soup into ramekins or bowls making sure not to fill too full. Gently place one to two croutons on the surface of the soup—don't push it in.

8. Gently lay cheese over the top, with some cheese overlapping the bowl.

9. Place in oven under broiler for 1 to 2 minutes until cheese is melting, toasted, and bubbling. Carefully remove from baking sheet and place on serving plate.

Butternut Squash with Apple

Autumn is a wonderful time in Wisconsin. The leaves are turning bright red, orange, and yellow. There's a chill in the air, and markets are filled with autumn fruits and vegetables. This soup showcases all that is wonderful about fall. It's so good that my friend asked a local restaurant to serve this soup at her bridal shower. It's fancy enough for company and simple enough to make for a weeknight supper. This quick soup can be prepared in 45 minutes or less.

For the Soup:

2 slices bacon

1 tablespoon olive oil

½ medium onion, chopped fine (about ½ cup)

1 large leek, white and pale green parts washed well, and chopped fine (about 1 cup)

1 large garlic clove, minced

½ bay leaf

1 ¼ pounds butternut squash (one large/two small) seeded, peeled, and cut into 1-inch pieces (about 3 cups)

1 apple, peeled, cored, and chopped into ½-inch pieces (pick your favorite, mine is Cortland)

2 cups chicken stock

Dash of ground nutmeg

Salt (½–1 teaspoon depending on stock) and pepper (black or white and black)

½ cup water plus additional for thinning soup

2 tablespoons sour cream or crème fraîche

Garnishes:

Any or all of these toppings will be great on your soup: sour cream or crème fraîche, chopped unpeeled apple, crumbled cooked bacon.

1. In a large saucepan or stockpot, cook bacon until crisp. Place bacon on paper towels to drain grease. Blot, and then crumble when cool.

2. Drain bacon grease from the pan into a can or container for disposal. The crispy brown bits can stay in the bottom of the pan. Crumble bacon and set aside.

3. Add olive oil to the pan. Add onion, leek. Sauté until softened and translucent. Add the garlic and bay leaf. Cook 1 to 2 minutes.

4. Add squash, apple, the bay leaf, salt, pepper, nutmeg, and broth. Add ½ cup water. Simmer mixture, covered, until squash is very tender, about 15 minutes, and discard bay leaf.

5. In a blender, or with an immersion blender, carefully purée mixture in batches, transferring back to a clean saucepan, and add enough additional water or stock to thin soup to your favorite consistency.

6. Gently stir in sour cream or crème fraîche, and pepper to taste. Heat the soup over low heat until hot (do not boil).

7. Serve soup topped with additional sour cream/crème fraîche, crumbled bacon, and small pieces of freshly chopped apple.

TORTILLA CHICKEN SOUP

Adapted from Wolfgang Puck

Serves 4 to 6

Soup

2 ears fresh corn, husks removed (frozen will also work)

4 or 5 large garlic cloves, peeled

1 small onion, peeled, trimmed, and quartered

1 jalapeno pepper, trimmed and seeded

2 tablespoons corn oil

2 6-inch corn tortillas, cut into 1-inch squares

2 large ripe tomatoes (1 pound), peeled, seeded, and coarsely chopped or use canned whole peeled tomatoes

2 tablespoons tomato paste

2–3 teaspoons ground cumin

2 quarts chicken stock

1–2 cooked chicken breasts, skin and bones removed, chopped into bite-sized pieces

Salt and freshly ground black pepper

Garnish

2 corn tortillas (or more!)

1 ripe avocado

½ cup grated Cheddar cheese

¼ cup chopped fresh cilantro leaves

Chopped red onion

1. Using a large knife, carefully cut the kernels off the corncobs and set aside, reserving the cobs. It's easiest to stand the corn on end and slice down toward the cutting board. You may want to cut the end of the cob so it will stand easily without slipping.

2. Using a food processor fitted with the steel blade, or a large knife, coarsely chop the garlic, onion, jalapeno pepper, and corn kernels. Set vegetables aside. Do not over-process the vegetables. You'll want some texture.

3. In a stockpot, heat the oil. Add the squares of tortillas and cook over low heat until they are slightly crisp. (Don't remove from the pot.)

4. Stir in the chopped vegetables and cook just until the vegetables are coated with the oil and slightly limp and the onions are translucent. Do not brown.

5. Add the tomatoes, the tomato paste, and 2 teaspoons of the cumin and continue to simmer for about 10 minutes.

6. Slowly pour in the stock, add the corncobs, and cook uncovered at a low boil/simmer until the soup is reduced by one third.

7. Carefully remove and discard the corn cobs and puree about one third of the soup, in batches, in a blender or food processor until smooth. Return to a clean pot and season with salt, pepper, and

---

TIP! I can't tell you how many times I've gone to our pantry to get a can of whole tomatoes only to find puree or sauce. Or, if it's winter and a recipe calls for fresh tomatoes, the tomatoes in the store are bleak at best. If this happens, don't fret. I often substitute and intermix tomato products. If I need puree, I use the food processor and some whole peeled tomatoes and make puree. If a have a can of tomato sauce, I may add it in place of diced tomatoes. Most of the time, I can't tell the difference. Sometimes the outcome is better. If you need more tomato flavor, add some tomato paste. Tomato paste can be diluted with water to make a lighter puree in a pinch. Just make sure the volume is about the same.

The Little French Bakery Cookbook

additional cumin to taste. Add the chopped, cooked chicken and simmer the soup until the chicken is heated through.

For the Tortilla Chips:

1. Preheat the oven or toaster oven to 350°F. Cut the tortillas into thin (¼–½ inch) strips and arrange on a small baking tray.

2. Bake until the strips are crisp, 10 to 15 minutes. Peel and dice the avocado. Grate cheddar cheese.

3. To serve, ladle the soup into six to eight warm soup bowls and garnish with the baked tortilla strips, Cheddar cheese, and chopped cilantro. Serve immediately.

TOMATO BISQUE SOUP

At my Little French Bakery Cooking School, classes break for lunch and enjoy a leisurely meal together. For our winter classes, this soup is often on the menu. There was a French restaurant group in Madison, Wisconsin, called the Baker's Rooms and Ovens of Brittany. I've adapted the recipe to lighten it up. It's warm, comforting, and can be as chunky or smooth as you like. Serve it with a big salad and some crusty bread.

Makes 6 servings

For the Soup:

½ stick butter, unsalted

2 tablespoons olive oil

⅓ cup flour

1 quart milk (2 percent works great)

½ cup heavy cream (optional)

1 green pepper, diced

1 cup diced celery

1½ cups finely chopped onion

1 clove garlic, minced

⅓ cup honey

3 28-ounce cans whole peeled tomatoes, chopped (with juice)

1–2 fresh tomatoes (if available), peeled, seeded, and chopped (see tip)

2 tablespoons dried basil or 6 tablespoons fresh, finely chopped

1–2 dashes hot pepper sauce

1 pinch cayenne pepper

1. In a saucepan, over medium heat, melt one stick of butter. Be careful not to let it brown.

2. Add the flour and whisk quickly to make a roux. Allow the mixture to cook for about 2 minutes, then slowly add the milk, and cream (if you're using).

3. Whisk constantly over low heat. After about 10 minutes, the mixture will thicken. Don't let it boil. Set aside.

4. In another larger pan, heat the olive oil over medium heat. Add the onions and green pepper. Cook until the onions are translucent, then add the garlic. Cook one to two minutes.

5. Add the tomatoes, honey, hot sauce, cayenne, and basil. Mix well, and simmer for 30 minutes.

6. To finish, add the white sauce, mix, and adjust seasonings with more cayenne or hot pepper sauce, salt, and pepper. If you prefer a less chunky texture, the soup can be pureed in batches, or use an immersion blender directly in the stockpot. Ladle into soup bowls and enjoy!

TIP! To peel and seed a tomato, bring two quarts of water to a boil in a medium/large saucepan. With a paring knife, make a small X in the skin on the bottom of each tomato. Have another bowl of cold water standing by. When the water reaches a boil, carefully add the tomatoes to the water. Boil for 30 seconds. Remove tomatoes from the boiling water and place into the cold water. When cool enough to handle, the skins should slip off easily. Slice tomato in half top to bottom. Slide fingers into seed clusters, and push out into compost/waste bowl. The remaining tomato pulp can be chopped or squished in your fingers and added to your recipe.

chapter ten

THE BREAKFAST CLASS

MORAVIAN SUGAR CAKE

Moravian settlers arrived in the United States near Bethlehem, Pennsylvania, in the 1700s. Sugar cake was a part of early Easter celebrations, and it also was enjoyed around the Christmas holidays. My parents and grandparents were Moravian. There are many church cookbooks with recipes for Sugar Cake. Here is mine.

Makes three 8×8 inch pans

1 cup sugar

1½ cup butter, melted

1 teaspoon salt

2¼-ounce packages active dry yeast

1 cup warm water (100–105°F)

1 cup hot mashed potatoes

2 eggs, slightly beaten

5–6 cups flour

1½ cup brown sugar (light)

5 teaspoons cinnamon

1. Add yeast to warm water.

2. Combine sugar, salt, eggs, 1 cup butter. Add in potatoes and add flour 1 cup at a time. Add in yeast/water. Beat until smooth.

3. Place in well-buttered bowl and allow to rise until doubled, about 1 to 2 hours.

4. Preheat your oven to 350°F.

5. Using three 8×8s or two 9×13 pans, press dough into pans with your fingertips.

6. Cover the dough with plastic wrap and allow it to rise in a draft-free place until doubled.

7. Remove the plastic wrap. Make dimples in dough, and sprinkle with brown sugar and cinnamon mixture. Drizzle with ½ cup butter.

8. Bake in preheated 350°F oven for 20 to 30 minutes or until bottom is golden. The cake should spring back when lightly pressed, and a toothpick inserted into the center should come out clean. Serve the Sugar Cake warm or at room temperature.

Big Fluffy Cinnamon Rolls

There are cinnamon rolls, and then there are cinnamon rolls. I love to teach this class. Students leave with huge pans of billowy rolls for family and friends. I know it can be intimidating to make bread from scratch. This dough is very forgiving and a great way to jump into the world of yeast and breads.

For the Dough:

2 packages active dry yeast (15 gm)

1 cup warm water (about 105–110°F)

⅔ cup granulated sugar, plus 1 pinch for proofing the yeast

1 cup warm milk (not hotter than 110°F)

⅔ cup butter

2 teaspoons salt

2 eggs, loosened

7½ cups all-purpose flour

1–2 tablespoons vegetable oil for oiling bowl

For the Filling:

1 cup butter, melted (divided)

1¾ cup granulated sugar (divided)

3 tablespoons ground cinnamon (the best you can find)

Optional Add-ins:

1½ cups chopped walnuts or pecans

1½ cups raisins or currants

1. Start your yeast by placing it in a small bowl with the water and a pinch of sugar. The yeast should start to foam within 5 minutes.

2. In another bowl, add the flour, milk, sugar, salt, eggs, and contents of yeast bowl. The dough will be shaggy and slightly sticky.

3. Turn the bowl onto the lightly floured counter. Cover with the bowl and rest the dough for 5 minutes. This will allow the flour to absorb the liquid and make for less kneading time.

4. Knead the dough for 5 to 10 minutes or until a gluten window forms (as explained in Chapter Two).

TIP! The best method for kneading is to pull the dough, fold it over, lift, flip, and slam/slap the dough on the counter. Try not to tear the dough as you're pulling, but stretch the dough. This motion will develop the gluten and create a wonderful structure. Don't add more flour unless you really need to. As the dough develops, it will require less flour and the stickiness will improve.

---

5. Pour about 1 tablespoon of vegetable oil a large bowl, and wipe oil around the bowl with your fingers or a paper towel. Not too much, but a generous swipe.

6. Shape the dough into the ball, by folding the edges to the middle. When you flip it over, you'll have a nice smooth side. Place the dough in the bowl smooth side down. Spin the dough three times and flip to cover with oil.

7. Cover the bowl with plastic wrap and place in comfortably warm place. Not too warm, draft-free is more important. Wait until the dough has doubled in size. This will take approximately 1 to 1½ hours. It will take longer if your room is cool, or the water and milk you used were cool.

8. While the dough is rising, mix together the sugar and cinnamon for the filling.

9. When you're ready to assemble the rolls, gently turn the dough out onto the countertop. Be gentle. Roll the dough into a 15x24 inch rectangle.

10. Using your hands, pour one half of the melted butter on the dough. Try to keep the butter from getting too close to the edge. Keep about ½-1 inch clear of butter and filling.

11. Sprinkle the sugar and cinnamon mixture on the butter. Starting on the long side, roll the dough away from you. I find that I need to pick up the roll of dough and help it go "up and over" rather than pushing the dough so that filling squishes out. Some find it easier to start on the far side and roll toward themselves. Either way is fine.

12. Using a large serrated knife, slice the dough into 12 to 15 pieces. The width of the slice will be the height of the roll. Remember, they are also going to expand in height and girth. In a 13×9 inch baking pan, pour ½ cup of the melted butter, and for an 8-inch pan, ¼ cup butter.

13. Sprinkle 1/4 cup sugar on top of the butter. Do not mix or stir.

14. Place the rolls in the pans cut sides down. Don't overcrowd. There may be a little space between the rolls, but they may also be touching.

15. Gently cover with plastic wrap or kitchen towel and let them rise again until doubled. This is can be hard to judge. It will take about 45 minutes.

16. As the rolls are rising, preheat your oven to 350°F.

17. When the rolls have risen, place pans in the oven. You may want to put the pan on a baking sheet to catch any drips of sugar and butter from the rolls.

18. Bake 25 to 30 minutes until the rolls are lightly golden brown. The center of the rolls will be the last part to finish baking.

19. Remove from the oven and cool and frost.

20. You can also cool completely, cover tightly in foil, and freeze for up to 3 months. To defrost, transfer to refrigerator overnight. To serve, place the pan back in a 250°F oven for 20 minutes to rewarm the rolls.

21. If you'd like to make a double batch, double all ingredients, and shape the dough into a 14×36 inch rectangle. The rolls will be the same size, but you'll have more of them.

TIP! If the edges of your rolls or bread are getting too brown, cover the pan with aluminum foil. This allows the rolls to bake without further browning. If you test for doneness using an instant-read thermometer, the temperature should be 180–200°F.

The Little French Bakery Cookbook

Cinnamon Roll Icing

Icing is a personal preference. I like to serve the rolls in big squares with the icing on the side. It's a plate with ribbons of rolls with icing dip. While a simple glaze of powdered sugar and milk will make a pretty glaze, here's the dreamy, fluffy dip. This recipe doubles well if you'd like more icing.

2 sticks butter or margarine (room temperature)

1 8-ounce package cream cheese (room temperature)

1 pound powdered sugar

1 teaspoon lemon juice

1 teaspoon vanilla extract

1. In a mixing bowl, beat together the butter and cream cheese. Add the powdered sugar, in small amounts to combine.

2. Continue beating for 10 to 12 minutes or until very light and smooth. Add the lemon juice and extract, mix to combine. Serve with the Fluffy Cinnamon Rolls.

CREAM CHEESE COFFEE CAKE SLICES

I had an "I want to have a bed and breakfast" phase. Many years ago, I thought it would be great fun to find a big house and open a B & B. My first step was to enroll us, Gary and me, in a university mini course for potential innkeepers. The class was really eye opening. There are many rules for opening and operating an inn. There are also things to think about such as privacy, personal time, who's going to get up early? Who will clean the rooms, and who will greet the guests? We pondered the idea, and even looked at a few properties. We never found the perfect spot, and in our search realized we might enjoy doing this for a short time, but not for the long term. Instead, we welcome friends to stay whenever they like. It's great fun for me to make "B & B style" breakfasts. This is one of the recipes I'd set aside for our B & B. It's also found its way into many recipe boxes from my cooking classes.

Makes three 12-inch coffee cakes, each sliced into about 10 pieces

1 8-ounce carton sour cream, or Greek yogurt

½ cup sugar

½ cup butter (1 stick), melted

1 teaspoon salt

2 ¼-ounce packages active dry yeast

½ cup warm water (not warmer than 105–110°F)

2 eggs, slightly beaten

4 cups flour

For the Filling:

2 8-ounce packages cream cheese, softened

¾ cup sugar

1 egg

⅛ teaspoon salt

2 teaspoons vanilla

For the Glaze:

2 cups confectioners' sugar

¼ cup milk

2 teaspoons vanilla

1. Heat sour cream in saucepan until it bubbles.

2. Remove from heat and add butter, sugar, and salt.

3. Dissolve yeast in water. Stir in sour cream mixture after cooled slightly. Transfer sour cream mixture to a mixing bowl. Add eggs.

4. Mix in flour, a bit at a time to make a soft dough.

5. Cover and chill overnight or at least 5 to 6 hours.

6. When ready to assemble, combine the cream cheese, sugar, egg, and vanilla and set aside. The filling can be made in a food processor or with a mixer. It should be smooth.

7. After the overnight chill, divide dough into three portions. Knead just four to five times on a lightly floured surface, then roll into a 12x10 inch rectangle.

8. Spread one third of the filling on each rectangle. Stay within ½ inch of the edge. Roll from long side and pinch edges to seal. Place seam side down on baking sheet lined with parchment paper.

9. Using a clean kitchen scissor or serrated knife, cut/snip four to five slashes or X's across the top.

10. Allow to rise about 1 hour (until doubled) in warm place.

11. Bake at 350°F for 15 to 20 minutes, or until golden brown.

12. While the pastry is baking prepare the glaze. Whisk the powdered sugar, vanilla, and milk together until very smooth.

13. Drizzle with glaze while warm. The glaze will run over the edges and puddle around the coffee cakes. Once the glaze has set, slice the coffee cakes into long slices on the diagonal and serve.

Strawberry Rhubarb Coffee Cake (Gluten Free)

The Little French Bakery gets many requests for gluten-free bakery items. At first I was resistant. I had trained in the land of white sugar and all-purpose flour. My gluten-free repertoire consisted of almond flour pastries and meringue-style treats rather than substitutions for wheat flour. In my search and desire to expand choices for friends and family members, I've found some really great gluten-free products. My very favorite is Cup4Cup. It really does substitute cup for a cup with all-purpose wheat flour in bakery items.

Makes one 8-inch coffee cake

For the Topping

8 tablespoons unsalted butter, or heart-healthy butter-like stick

1 cup all-purpose gluten-free flour (Bob's Red Mill and Cup4Cup are great)

½ teaspoon xanthan gum (if not using a baking mix)

¼ cup granulated sugar

⅓ cup packed light brown sugar

⅛ teaspoon salt

For the Batter

3–4 stalks fresh rhubarb, cut into tiny ¼-inch pieces

1–2 cups fresh strawberries, hulled and sliced (you can also substitute other fruits)

1¼ cup all-purpose gluten-free flour

½ teaspoon xanthan gum (reduce to ¼ teaspoon if using Cup4Cup)

¾ teaspoon baking powder

¼ teaspoon baking soda

¼ teaspoon salt

¾ cup granulated sugar

2 tablespoons butter, room temperature

4 tablespoons shortening

6 tablespoons plain Greek yogurt

3 large eggs, or equivalent of egg substitute

½ teaspoon vanilla extract

1. Preheat your oven to 350°F.

2. Grease and flour an 8-inch cake pan (round or square). Line the bottom with parchment paper.

3. Combine the topping ingredients and blend with a fork until just combined. Place in refrigerator until needed.

4. For the cake batter, in a small bowl, combine the fruits with the brown sugar and ¼ cup flour, stir and set aside.

5. In another bowl, mix the remaining flour, xanthan gum, baking powder, soda, salt, and ¾ cup granulated sugar. By hand or with a mixer (paddle attachment for Kitchen Aid) add the butter, shortening, and yogurt, and mix. Add the eggs one at a time and mix after each addition. Add vanilla, then fold in the fruit. The batter will be thick. Mix just until combined.

6. Scrape batter into the pan, smooth, and bake in preheated oven for 30 minutes. After the cake has been baking about 20 minutes, remove the topping from the refrigerator, and toss/fluff with a fork to create the crumbles.

7. Remove the cake from the oven, sprinkle on the topping, and return to the oven for another 20 to 30 minutes or until a toothpick inserted comes out clean or with just a few crumbs. Remove from the oven and cool completely, carefully turn out of pan, and remove parchment. Then return to plate or pedestal. Slice into squares or wedges.

COOKING SCHOOL GRANOLA

Every cooking class starts with breakfast. We gather around the table and get to know each other over coffee, a breakfast pastry, some yogurt, and Cooking School Granola. It can be layered to make yogurt and fruit parfaits, served with milk, or nibbled right off the baking sheet. It freezes very well. You can easily double the recipe for a larger batch.

Makes about 6 cups or 8 generous servings

¼ cup vegetable oil

¼ cup maple syrup

2 tablespoons molasses

1 cup sliced almonds, or a mixture of chopped walnuts and almonds

½ cup shredded coconut (sweetened)

2½ cups rolled oats (old-fashioned style)

½ cup raisins

½ cup dried cherries

½ cup chopped dates or dried plums

Other optional add-ins:

Chopped dried pineapple, dried apricots, banana chips, additional nuts

1. Preheat your oven to 350°F.

2. Mix all the ingredients together in a mixing bowl, by hand, or with a spatula/spoon. Be careful not to crush or break up the mixture too much. Spread the granola onto a baking sheet or into a baking pan.

3. Bake about 20 minutes, and then stir to bring the less browned granola to the top. Return to the oven and bake until golden brown. Stir about every 10 to 15 minutes. Total baking time is about 40 to 50 minutes.

4. When the granola is golden brown, remove the pan from the oven and cool on a baking rack. When cool, stir and break up any large pieces. Add dried fruits and other add-ins. Store in an airtight container or freezer bag.

CINNAMON COFFEE CAKE

Here's a recipe you can make at the spur of the moment with ingredients you almost always have on hand. I've made this in round or heart-shaped springform pans for easy removal to a serving plate. Add a handful of blueberries into the batter for an extra treat.

For the Coffee Cake

¼ cup shortening

¼ cup granulated sugar

2 eggs

2 cups all-purpose flour

1 teaspoon salt

1 tablespoon baking powder

1½ teaspoon ground cinnamon

1 cup milk

For the Topping:

1½ teaspoons ground cinnamon

½ cup granulated sugar

2–3 teaspoons melted butter

1. Preheat your oven to 375°F. Grease and flour the springform pan, set aside.

2. In a separate bowl combine the flour, salt, sugar, baking powder, and cinnamon. Whisk to combine and lighten.

3. Starting with the flour mixture, alternate adding one third of flour mixture then milk to the sugar/shortening mixture. Mix to combine after each addition. Beat another 15 to 30 seconds to combine.

4. Pour the batter into the pan.

5. In a small bowl, combine the topping ingredients. The mixture should feel like wet sand and be dry enough to sprinkle. Sprinkle the topping over the batter.

6. Place in the preheated oven and bake for 40 minutes. A toothpick inserted into the center should be dry and without crumbs when pulled out. Cool for 5 to 10 minutes, and then carefully remove the springform ring. Cool for another 10 to 15 minutes, then serve.

chapter eleven

OUR FAMILY FAVORITES

JAMBALAYA WITH SPICY SAUCE

Chef Paul Prudhomme's recipes and books are amazing. His words walk you through Cajun recipes without fail. In the middle of winter, there's nothing better than a plate of jambalaya filled with tender chicken and shrimp. This spicy rice dish can be made with chicken, shrimp, sausage, or all three. The trinity of Cajun cooking is onion, celery, and green pepper. These vegetables are the building blocks for almost any Creole dish. I've adapted Chef Prudhomme's several jambalaya recipes to create a version our family and friends always enjoy. The Spicy Cajun Tomato Sauce adds a nice touch.

Serves 4 to 6

For the spice mix:

3 bay leaves

1½ teaspoon salt

½–1 teaspoon cayenne pepper

1 teaspoon ground white pepper

1½ teaspoon dried oregano leaves

1 teaspoon ground black pepper

¾ dried thyme leaves

1 teaspoon garlic powder

¼ teaspoon paprika

Mix all the spice ingredients together, and set aside.

For the jambalaya:

1 large onion, minced

3 stalks (about 1 cup) celery, finely chopped

1 green pepper, seeded and finely chopped

2 tablespoons olive oil

4 boneless/skinless chicken breasts, fat trimmed and cut into 1-inch cubes

¼–½ pound sliced kielbasa (like coins) or cured ham, chopped (optional)

2 dozen shrimp, peeled and deveined (frozen-precooked or fresh)

2 cloves garlic, minced

2 cups chicken stock (preferably homemade)

2 cups uncooked rice

4–6 green onions/scallions finely chopped (white and light green parts)

1 small can tomato paste

1 small can whole peeled tomatoes or 3–4 medium fresh tomatoes peeled and chopped

1. Preheat your oven to 350°F.

2. In a large stockpot or enamel dutch oven, heat olive oil over medium heat. Add the green peppers, celery, and onions and cook until the vegetables are beginning to soften and the onions are translucent.

3. Scrape the bottom of the pan well, increase the heat to medium/high, and add the chicken. Toss and stir the mixture constantly until the chicken is mostly cooked. This will be about 6 minutes. Reduce the heat to medium.

4. Add the spice mix and the garlic. Scrape the pan often to prevent the spices from burning.

5. Mix ¼ cup of the tomato paste in ½ cup water. Add to the pan. If you're using canned tomatoes, drain and squeeze four tomatoes between your fingers and into the mixture.

6. If using chopped, add the tomatoes. Add the chicken stock and bring the mixture to a boil. Stir in one half of the green onions and the rice.

7. Add the shrimp.

The Little French Bakery Cookbook

8. Carefully pour the mixture into a baking pan. I use an oval 2-quart pan.

9. You can also use an 8x8 cake pan. Cover the pan with foil, taking care to carefully seal the edges by pinching the foil over the edge of the pan.

10. Bake 35 to 40 minutes until the rice is tender. Serve garnished with the remaining green onion. Remove the bay leaves (or caution your guests).

SPICY CAJUN TOMATO SAUCE

This sauce is great on omelets and pasta. It's also a great addition to the jambalaya.

1 bay leaf

½ teaspoon dried thyme

½ teaspoon dried oregano

½ teaspoon salt

½ teaspoon dried basil

½ teaspoon ground black pepper

½ teaspoon ground white pepper

1 teaspoon paprika

¼–½ teaspoon cayenne pepper

Mix all the ingredients together and set aside

For the Sauce:

2 tablespoons butter

1 tablespoon olive oil

1 small/medium onion, chopped

2 stalks celery, chopped (about ½–¾ cup)

1 green pepper chopped (seeds and core removed)

3 cloves garlic, chopped

1½ cups chicken stock (preferably homemade) or organic/low-salt

¼ cup tomato paste (use the remaining paste from the jambalaya), mixed with ¾ cup water

1 teaspoon brown or white sugar

2–4 dashes hot sauce, such as Tabasco

1. Melt the butter in a saucepan. Add the olive oil.

2. Add the green pepper, onions, and celery. Cook until the onions are translucent and the vegetables are beginning to soften.

3. Add the stock and tomato paste. Stir in the sugar and hot sauce.

4. Bring to a boil, then reduce to a simmer until the vegetables are tender and the sauce is reduced by about one quarter, about 30 minutes.

ANTIPASTO SALAD WITH SALAMI

This hearty pasta salad is a great picnic meal. Look for interesting pasta shapes with nooks and crannies to hold the dressing.

Serves 8 to 10

1 pound rotini or fusilli or any corkscrew-shaped pastas

2 garlic cloves

2 tablespoons Dijon-style mustard

½ cup red-wine vinegar

2½ tablespoons balsamic vinegar

1 tablespoon water

½ cup vegetable oil

1 ounce (½ cup) sun-dried tomatoes

½ pound smoked gouda, cut into ½-inch cubes

½ pound fresh mozzarella, cut into ½-inch cubes

1 1-pound can garbanzo beans, drained and rinsed

1 small can artichoke hearts, cut in half (smaller bites)

1–2 tablespoons capers

3½ ounces sliced hard salami, cut into ½-inch julienne strips

10–20 bottled small peperoncini (pickled Tuscan peppers)

1 cup cherry tomatoes cut in half

½ teaspoon dried hot red pepper flakes

1 cup loosely packed fresh flat-leafed parsley leaves, minced

1. Start boiling salted water in a large pan. Cook the rotini until it is tender. Rinse with cold water until cool, drain, and set aside.

2. Using a food processor or blender, blend the garlic, mustard, vinegars, water, oil, and salt to taste until the dressing is smooth and well combined.

3. In a very large bowl toss the pasta with dressing and stir in the sun-dried tomatoes, artichoke hearts, mozzarella, gouda, garbanzos, salami, peppers, the red pepper flakes, capers, and parsley. Gently fold in the dressing.

4. Add tomatoes and more chopped parsley for garnish.

5. Chill the salad, covered, for 1 hour. The salad may be made 2 days in advance and kept covered and chilled.

SALADE NIÇOISE

When I arrive in Paris, I'm always a bit jet lagged. I've found I recover much faster and feel better the first day of my trip if I keep plenty of good food in my stomach. Protein and vegetables seem to be the cure for me. Next to my favorite hotel is a cafe that makes one of the best Salade Nicoise I've ever had. Each ingredient is given special attention before it's placed on the large salad plate.

I prepare the eggs just before serving so they're still just a bit warm. Prepare the salad on a big platter and serve it at the table with a little extra dressing for passing. Pair with a glass of wine and crusty bread.

Serves 6

2 large heads Boston and Romaine lettuce leaves, or assorted greens washed and dried

1 pound green beans, cooked and refreshed in ice water

2 shallots, finely sliced

½ to ⅔ cup French Vinaigrette Dressing

Salt and freshly ground pepper

3–4 ripe red tomatoes, cut into wedges (or 10–12 cherry tomatoes, halved)

3–4 small red potatoes or 1–2 large russet

4 large eggs, hard boiled and quartered lengthwise

1 red bell pepper, seeded and sliced lengthwise ¼–½ inch strips

Two 3-ounce cans chunk tuna, preferably oil-packed

4–6 anchovy fillets

½ cup small black Niçoise-type olives

2–3 tablespoons capers, drained

3 tablespoons minced fresh parsley

1. In a medium pot, place the potatoes in cold water. Bring to a boil, and boil for 20 to 25 minutes until the potatoes are fork tender. Drain, and rinse under cold water. When cool enough to handle, peel and slice into small wedges or 1-inch cubes.

2. Place in a bowl and sprinkle with ½ teaspoon salt and ½ pepper. Drizzle with 2 tablespoons dressing, and set aside.

3. To prepare the beans, bring 2 quarts salted water to a boil. Add beans and cook for 6 to 8 minutes, until desired tenderness. Drain beans, and place in a bowl of water filled with ice cubes. This will keep the beans bright green.

4. Drain the green beans and pat dry. Toss with one half of the shallots, a few spoonfuls of vinaigrette, and salt and pepper.

5. Drizzle the wedges of tomato with a few spoonfuls of vinaigrette.

6. To assemble, arrange the lettuce leaves on a large platter or in a shallow bowl. Place the tuna in the center of the platter, drizzle with dressing. Then, arrange a mound of beans at either end, with tomatoes and potatoes clustered on the opposite side.

7. Place the eggs, olives, and green peppers in clusters in the corners. Drizzle with more vinaigrette. Top with the anchovies and a sprinkle of chopped parsley and shallots.

The Little French Bakery Cookbook

TIP! To make hard-boiled eggs, start with a saucepan of cold water. Add the eggs in a single layer. Be sure the eggs are covered by at least 1 inch of water. Bring the water to a boil. Reduce heat, and simmer for 2 minutes. Cover the pan, turn off the heat and rest the eggs for 20 minutes. Transfer the eggs to a bowl of cool water. When the eggs are cool enough to handle, they can be peeled.

French Vinaigrette Dressing

¼ cup red wine vinegar

2–3 teaspoons Dijon mustard

½ cup canola oil

½ cup olive oil

1 clove garlic, smashed with salt to make a paste.

1. In a small bowl, whisk together the vinegar and mustard.

2. Add the garlic.

3. Whisk in oils with a small whisk or a fork.

4. Adjust salt/pepper as desired. Re-whisk just before serving.

Mushroom Risotto with Grilled Salmon

I don't remember the first time I made risotto, but it was years ago. It's on my dear friend Kim's list of things to eat every time she visits. The recipe is part of my Comfort Foods class. The secret is low to medium heat and plenty of time to stir the rice to create the creamy consistency. I like to serve the risotto on top of a grilled salmon filet. You can also add shrimp, asparagus, or other seasonal vegetables.

Serves 4

1 tablespoon butter

1 tablespoon olive oil

1 medium onion, finely chopped

1 pinch saffron

1–2 teaspoons salt (you will not need as much salt if you are using Parmesan cheese or salted chicken broth)

1 teaspoon freshly ground black pepper

1 cup dry white wine

1½ cups Arborio or Carnaroli rice

6–8 cups chicken stock (preferably homemade) or organic low-salt

1 cup fresh or frozen green peas

1 cup Parmesan or Grana Padano cheese, finely grated plus more for passing

1 cup fresh mushrooms, thinly sliced

1 tablespoon heavy cream (optional)

1. In a saucepan, heat the broth with the saffron to a boil, and then reduce the heat to a simmer. In another large pan or shallow dutch oven, melt the butter, add the oil, and heat over medium heat.

2. Add the onion and cook until it is tender and translucent. Be careful to keep the onions from browning.

3. Add the rice. Stir constantly to coat the rice with the oil/butter. The rice should not brown, but will sizzle and make popping sounds.

The Little French Bakery Cookbook

4. Carefully add the wine. The rice will spit and pop. Stir constantly over medium/low heat until the wine has been absorbed.

5. Using a ladle, spoon some of the stock over the rice, just to cover. Stir frequently until most of the liquid is absorbed. Add more stock, continuing to stir.

6. Continue stirring and adding stock until the rice is plump and tender to the bite. You may not need all the stock. If you use all the stock and need more, you can add more wine, or some water. The stirring process will take approximately 30 minutes.

7. As you add the last cup or two of stock, add the peas. When the rice is tender, and most of the stock has been added, add the mushrooms and the cheese.

8. Stir to melt the cheese into the risotto and warm the mushrooms through.

9. Just before serving add heavy cream and stir. Adjust salt and pepper to taste. I usually add more black pepper as a personal preference.

10. Serve in large bowls over grilled salmon, chicken, or seafood. Pass extra cheese.

STOVETOP GRILLED SALMON

One of my favorite pans is my grill pan. I use it for making pork tenderloins, salmon, bacon, or even quick chicken breasts. It heats quickly and even makes grill marks as if I were cooking outside. The raised ridges keep the meats from sitting in any fat.

Serves 4

4 4-ounce salmon filets
½ tablespoon olive oil
Salt and pepper

1. Heat the grill pan over high heat. Blot the filets to remove any excess moisture. Using a paper towel or pastry brush, carefully brush with olive oil.

2. Place the fish skin side down on the grill pan. Salt and pepper the top side while the salmon cooks. Cook for 4 minutes over medium/high heat then flip the fish. You should see the color changing about halfway up the side of the filet.

3. Sprinkle with salt and pepper. You'll be able to see the color changing on the side of the filets as they cook through. Cook another 3 to 4 minutes. Remove the filets from the heat to a plate and cover tightly with aluminum foil. Rest for 10 minutes.

TIP! If you're trying to figure out if your pan is ready to add meat, here's a tip. Heat the pan, then hold your palm over the pan about 4 to 6 inches away from the cooking surface. If you can hold your hand in place for more than 3 seconds, the pan is not ready. When you can't keep your hand over the pan for 3 seconds, it's ready to add the meat. Once you've placed the meat or fish in the pan, don't attempt to move it for at least 2 to 3 minutes. If it's too soon, the meat will stick and tear.

chapter twelve

TARTS AND PIES

making tart aux pommes

When students come to a tart class, their eyes light up when they learn we're going to make this tart. It's such an icon of French pastry. For French apple desserts, Golden Delicious apples are very popular. They keep their shape as they bake, don't give off too much juice, and have a sweet, delicate flavor. I had never baked with this variety until pastry school. I live in the land of Cortlands and MacIntosh, but seek out Golden Delicious for this tart.

Another interesting thing I learned while working with apples is the French don't mix apples and cinnamon the way Americans do. There are a few recipes with cinnamon, but not many.

While we were watching the chef demonstrate this recipe, a student raised her hand and asked the chef if we could add cinnamon to the simmering apples? "Pourquoi?" he asked. "C'est tarte aux pomme. Si vous ajoutez la cannelle, ce ne sera pas tarte aux pomme, mais un autre dessert." He was telling us if we add cinnamon, then it won't be a *tarte aux pomme*, but another dessert. He went on to explain that each French pastry is given a name. Every pastry chef learns to make the pastry exactly the same way. That way, customers always know what to expect. If you change the pastry, then you should have a new name. This makes sense to me. When customers call to order a pastry, I can feel confident the pastry I'm making will be what they're expecting. There's something comforting to me about tradition.

TART AUX POMMES

Makes 1 tart

1 recipe Pâte Brisée	1 lemon
6–7 Golden Delicious apples	½ cup sugar
4 tablespoons unsalted butter, divided	Nappage apricot glaze (or apricot preserves, heated and strained)

1. Preheat your oven to 350°F.

2. Line a 10-inch tart ring with the pâte brisée and chill.

3. Peel, core, and chop four of the apples and place in a skillet or large dutch oven. Add ⅔ cup water, 3 tablespoons butter, and sugar.

4. Bring the apples to a simmer over medium heat. Cook, stirring occasionally, until the apples will squish under the pressure of your spoon, but are still retaining their shape.

5. The liquid should be mostly evaporated. The sugar will cause the apples to caramelize a bit.

6. Remove the pan from the heat to cool the apples. You may wish to transfer the apples to a plate or cool baking pan to speed the cooling process.

7. With the remaining apples, carefully peel and core. Try not to make deep cuts into the apples. Immediately, rub the peeled apples with lemon juice to reduce browning. Cut one apple in half top to bottom and lay cut side down. Slice ¹⁄₁₆–⅛ inch slices, working stem end to blossom end. Try to make the slices as uniform as possible. Repeat with the remaining apples. Squeeze a bit of lemon juice over the slices.

8. Transfer the cooled cooked apples into the center of the tart crust. Spread the apples to the edges, but keep a mound of apple compote in the center, about ¾-1 inch deep.

9. Starting at the outer edge, place an apple slice with an end touching the crust, and round side slightly diagonal into the tart. Place the next slice so that it overlaps the seed side of the first slice and hides the end near the crust. Repeat until you've made a circle around the tart. You'll tuck the last slice under the first. Make another ring of slices with about one third of the second ring of slices overlapping the first. In the center, place some small slices to make a tiny flower, or simply fill the space.

10. Melt the remaining butter. With a pastry brush, carefully blot and dab the slices. Be very gentle as the brush can easily disturb the apples. If it's too tricky, better to have less butter than messy apples.

11. Place the tart in the oven and bake 25 to 35 minutes or until the crust is deep golden brown. The edges of the apples will be deep golden as well.

12. Remove the tart from the oven, and cool. Heat the nappage and with a pastry brush, glaze the tart with the apricot glaze. Allow the tart to set for about 10 minutes, then serve.

FRANGIPANE TART WITH PEARS

People often ask me what my favorite pastry is to make, and eat. I usually reply that I enjoy all different kinds. But deep down, I have to admit, I do have a favorite. I love to make and eat this tart. It's the best on so many levels. The pears, the incredible almond cream, and the flaky, buttery tart crust. It's fun to make, too. The tart is very forgiving. If it droops a little on one side as it bakes, it just adds character to the rustic style of a tart. It's glazed with nappage, the shiny glaze to make it glisten and glimmer on any platter. I teach this tart in almost every tart class. Beginners are amazed as they peek in the oven and see the almond cream puffing between the slices of fruit. Everyone can be a star with this tart. I hope you enjoy this one as much as I do.

1 batch Pâte Brisée (see p. 22)

2 cans pears

nappage

creme fraiche for garnish

1 batch **Crème Amande** (Almond Cream) as follows:

⅔ cup (60 grams) almond flour

4 tablespoons (60 grams) butter, very soft but not melted

6 tablespoons (60 grams) sugar

1 egg

A few pinches of flour

1. Prepare the tart crust per the instructions in Chapter Two.

2. Lightly butter the inside edges of the tart pan. Roll and place the Pâte Brisée in the pan and cool in refrigerator while you prepare the other ingredients.

3. Preheat your oven to 350°F.

4. To prepare the almond cream, place butter and sugar in a small bowl. Using your fingers, mix the butter and sugar together. Add the almond flour and mix.

5. Add the egg and mix until combined. Add the vanilla and mix. If the mixture seems quite loose, dust with 1 to 2 teaspoons of flour. The mixture should be very soft and spreadable.

6. Remove the crust from the refrigerator. Scrape the cream from the bowl into the crust. Using an offset spatula or butter knife, spread an even layer on the crust. It will be approximately ¼ inch thick.

7. Remove six pear halves and place on a clean dry towel or paper towel to absorb extra syrup. Using a straight chef knife, slice the pear crosswise into thin slices. Keep the slices in the shape of the pear. Try to make the slices the same thickness, about ⅛ inch thick.

8. Now for the fun part. Using a knife or offset spatula, slide under the pear and pick up the whole half and place on the cream with the narrow part of the pear in the center of the tart, and the wider end pointing to the edge, like the minute hand on a clock. You'll have room for about six halves. Gently press on the slices toward the outer edge to make a fan of slices. You might push some of the cream, but don't worry. It will be fine.

9. Bake the tart for 25 to 35 minutes, until the cream is puffed and golden. The crust should also be golden brown.

10. Allow the tart to cool on the pan.

11. Heat the nappage, and carefully brush the pears and almond cream. Wait 5 to 10 minutes for the glaze to set.

12. Serve and enjoy. Crème fraîche makes a wonderful topping. Add a dollop just before serving, or pass in a pretty bowl or pitcher.

ALL-AMERICAN APPLE PIE WITH CRUMBLE TOP

If you've ever made a pie and the crust is ready before the apples are cooked and the top is burning, this is the recipe for you. All the components are made, baked, and assembled at the end with a short bake to combine all the flavors. I've adapted the Dutch Apple Pie recipe from *Cooks Illustrated*. I like the flavor of the Golden Delicious apples and the pâte brisée crust. If you'd like to give your pie a Wisconsin twist, serve it with a slice of Cheddar cheese and a scoop of vanilla ice cream.

For the crust:

One batch Pâte Brisée

1 egg for egg wash

For the apple filling:

4½–5 pounds Golden Delicious and Granny Smith apples (half and half)

¼ cup sugar

½ teaspoon cinnamon

¼ teaspoon salt

2 tablespoons unsalted butter

½ cup heavy cream

For the crumble topping:

1½ cups all-purpose flour

⅓ cup brown sugar

⅓ cup granulated sugar

1 tablespoon cornmeal

1 stick unsalted butter, melted

Ice cream and/or a slice of Cheddar cheese for each serving

1. Preheat your oven to 400°F.

2. Roll the dough into a 12-inch circle, then fit into a 9-inch pie pan. Line the crust with foil, and fill with uncooked beans or pie weights.

3. Bake for 15 to 20 minutes. Carefully lift the foil and weights from the crust, brush with egg wash, then return the crust to the oven to finish baking, about 15 more minutes, or until the crust is golden brown.

4. Remove from the oven to a cooking rack.

5. For the filling, peel, core, and dice the apples into ¼–½ inch pieces. Place the apples, butter, sugar, and spices in a large pan and cook until the apples are softened.

6. Transfer the apples to a bowl, keeping the juices in the pan.

7. Add the cream to the juices in the pan and cook until the mixture has thickened, about 5 minutes.

8. Place the apples in the crust, then pour the cream and juice mixture over the apples.

9. To finish, combine the crumble topping ingredients in a small bowl by hand. Place on a parchment, lined baking sheet and bake for about 5 to 7 minutes or until it's golden brown. Transfer the pan to a cooling rack. Slide the parchment off the pan, so the crumble can cool faster. When the crumble can be handled, sprinkle it over the apples.

10. To keep the pie from dripping onto your oven floor, set it back on the parchment and onto the baking sheet. It's much easier to handle. Place the baking sheet in the oven and bake the pie for an additional 10 to 15 minutes, until the crumble is very golden brown. Cool your pie and serve.

FRUIT GALETTE

Nearly every cafe, bistro, and restaurant in Paris has a dessert cart or table. Desserts are proudly displayed as you pass to your table. In smaller cafes it's not uncommon to see galettes. Rather than shape the tart in a pan, the crust is rolled, cut in a circle and filled with fruit. The edge of the crust in rolled over to make a pretty edge, and to keep the juices in the center. Galettes are rustic and always a delicious finish to a meal.

Here's the first step in tart making. Make the galette any size, small or family sized. Don't worry about the pan, just make the dough, add the fruit, and bake. I like to use plums and peaches for a summery dessert topped with crème fraîche or ice cream.

Makes one 10-inch or two 6-inch galettes

1 batch Pâte Brisée

2–3 fresh, ripe peaches, pears, or plums

1 tablespoon granulated sugar

Apricot glaze or preserves (heated and strained)

1. Preheat your oven to 350°F.

2. Roll the tart dough to ⅛–¼ inch thick.

3. Using a pan lid, or free hand, cut into a circle. If you are making small tarts, cut both circles at once. Don't re-knead the dough. It will be tough and hard to roll the second time.

4. Transfer the dough onto a parchment-lined baking sheet.

5. Slice the fruit in wedges, and place closely in rings on the dough. Starting at one edge, fold ½ inch of the dough over, then move about 1 inch around, and fold. The dough will have a pretty folded edge.

6. Sprinkle with sugar, and place in the oven until the crust is deep golden brown, about 25 minutes. Remove from the oven, cool, and brush the fruit with warm apricot glaze. Wait at least 5 minutes for the glaze to set, and serve.

7. For an extra special galette, make Frangipane (Almond Cream). Use an offset spatula or the back of a spoon to spread the cream on the crust before adding the fruit. The cream will puff between the pieces of fruit and add a delicious layer of filling.

CHOCOLATE GANACHE TART

There were a few techniques I saw in school that amazed me. Things I thought were impossible. One was boiling milk and cream. Boiling cream was like waiting 30 minutes after eating before swimming. Someone told you not to do it, and you didn't want to find out what would happen if you didn't follow the advice.

Fast forward to pastry school. The chef poured a few cups of cream into a saucepan, started the stove top, and let it boil. What?! What is he doing? You can't boil cream! I'm sure I wasn't the only person in the group who was thinking that. He did it. Many times, quite successfully. He boiled milk, too. The biggest surprise was making pastry cream and boiling milk with sugar in it. No burned mess on the bottom of the pan, no skin on the surface. Who started the rumor you can't boil milk and cream?

Ganache is the product of emulsifying chocolate and liquid. Usually cream. When ganache is liquid it can be poured over cakes or used for dipping. When it's firmer it can be piped into the center of chocolate bonbons or rolled into truffles. When made correctly, it's smooth, and melts in your mouth. The best ganache is 50/50 chocolate to liquid by weight. Butter is often added for truffles to give the ganache a smooth, creamy texture.

The ganache tart is like eating a big truffle. The crust holds the poured ganache, and the glaze make the tart glisten. Hold the tart in the refrigerator, but bring out well before serving to warm a bit. Depending on your location, this could be 10 minutes or an hour. Use your favorite tasting and the best chocolate you can find. I like a dark chocolate just around 58 to 60 percent cocoa. It's not too bitter and has the perfect chocolate flavor to me.

In most cases, water touching chocolate leads to a disaster. Equipment with drops of water, or steam, is the enemy. The grainy sandlike damage to the chocolate is irreversible. This is called seizing. However, when you add more than a mist or drip of water, the chocolate will not seize. The amounts of water in these recipes will complement the chocolate and give a beautiful shine to the finished tart.

One recipe Pâte Brisée or Sweet Shortcrust (recipe follows), blind baked

For the Crust:

1¾ cups plus 2 tablespoons (200 grams) all-purpose flour

9 tablespoons (130 grams) butter

6 tablespoons plus 2 teaspoons (80 grams) sugar

⅛ teaspoon salt

1 large egg

1 egg for egg wash

1. Cut the butter into the flour; the bits of dough and butter should resemble the size of peas. Make a well and add the sugar, salt, and egg to the center. Mix well with your fingertips.

2. Using a pastry scraper or knives, cut the egg mixture into the flour/butter mixture.

3. Make a line of dough across the work surface in front of you and with the heel of your hand, smear the dough forward to combine. Gather the dough, and repeat. The dough should be combined with two to three passes. Gather the dough, shape into a disk, wrap, and chill for at least 20 minutes.

4. Preheat your oven to 350°F.

5. Roll the dough into a 12-inch disk, and fit into a 10-inch tart pan, placed on a baking sheet.

With a fork, make a few taps on the bottom to keep the tart bottom flat while baking.Line the tart pan with foil. Fill with pie weights or uncooked beans. Place in oven and bake for 15 to 20 minutes. Carefully lift the foil and beans. Whisk the egg in a small bowl with a fork, and with a pastry brush, brush the tart with the egg wash. Take extra care to dab in the holes from the fork tines. Place the tart crust back in the oven and continue baking until deep golden brown, approximately 15 more minutes. Remove from the oven and cool completely.

For Ganache:

1⅔ cups (350 grams) heavy cream

3 cups (350 grams) chocolate, chopped

5½ tablespoons (80 grams) butter, cool room temperature

1. In a heavy-bottomed saucepan, heat the cream to boiling.

2. Place the chocolate in a mixing bowl. Pour the hot cream over the chocolate. Stir to distribute the cream throughout the chocolate. Let the mixture rest for 2 to 3 minutes.

3. Starting in the center, quickly stir the mixture. You are emulsifying the two ingredients as you would a salad dressing. As you see the smooth ganache forming in the center, gradually increase your circle to include more and more of the chocolate and cream. When the mixture is nearly combined, add the butter and stir until the ganache is well combined and glossy.

4. The finished ganache should be smooth and shiny. Pour the ganache into the cooled tart crust and allow to cool to room temperature. You may place the tart in the refrigerator if desired. When the ganache is firm (about the texture of a truffle), make the glaze. Before adding the glaze be sure the tart is not too cold.

For the Glaze:

1¼ cups (125 grams) chocolate

3 tablespoons (60 grams) light corn syrup

4 tablespoons (60 grams) water

1. Heat the chocolate and water over a water bath or in a microwave. Stir to combine.

2. Add the corn syrup and stir. The mixture should be smooth and glossy.

3. Pour the glaze onto the ganache. It's best to pour onto the center of the tart, and allow the glaze to spread over the surface. Garnish the edge of the tart with nuts or berries.

FRESH STRAWBERRY TARTLETTES

If you've been to France in the spring, you've seen the beautiful strawberry tarts in the patisserie cases. The fruit is perfectly ripened, and placed on top of a pillow of creme pâtissiere. The crowning touch is a generous glaze of nappage, or apricot glaze.

Nappage is magic. It can take a pretty yet humble tart and make it stunning. Nappage adds a very slight golden color, a touch of sweetness, and a glistening finish to help keep the pastry fresh in the pastry case.

The first time we used nappage, we were simply amazed. Where had this been all our lives? Soon it became second nature to heat the nappage and carefully brush it on our finished work. In our quiet silliness, we realized we were nappaging with nappage. So was it a noun or a verb? We assumed both. It also became a salutation. At the end of a long tired day, it wasn't unusual to bid a classmate goodbye, with a smirk and a "nappage!"

Makes 4 to 6 small or 1 10-inch tart

1 recipe Pâte Brisée, blind baked

1 egg

1–2 pints fresh, ripe strawberries, stems removed

1 recipe pastry cream

1 cup nappage, or apricot preserves, heated and strained

To assemble:

Fill the tart shells with pastry cream, then top with strawberries, top side down. Heat nappage and brush onto berries. Allow about 5 minutes for the glaze to set, and serve. The tarts should be assembled close to serving time to keep the crust crisp and the berries from juicing when in contact with the pastry cream.

CLEMENTINE CURD TART WITH BERRIES

Lemon and lime are delicious as a filling between simple cakes, inside a cupcake, or spooned into a tart shell and topped with fresh fruit. I like to pair raspberries with lemon curd and blueberries with lime curd. Any citrus juice will work well, even grapefruit. Follow the recipe for fresh strawberry tarts, substituting citrus curd for the pastry cream.

Makes 1 tart

1 recipe Pâte Brisée, blind baked

Raspberries, Blueberries, and/or Blackberries

1 recipe Clementine Curd

For the Curd:

6 egg yolks, from large eggs

1 cup sugar

⅓ cup freshly squeezed Clementine orange juice

Juice of ½ lemon

1 tablespoon cornstarch

1 tablespoon orange zest, finely minced

½ cup (1 stick) cold butter, cut into 8–10 pieces

1. In a mixing bowl, whisk the egg yolks and sugar together.

2. In another small cup, mix the cornstarch into the lemon juice.

3. Pour the mixtures into a saucepan and cook over low/medium heat, stirring constantly but gently, until the mixture is thickened, about 10 minutes. The curd should coat the back of a wooden spoon.

4. Stir the butter into the curd piece by piece to combine.

5. Pour the curd into a bowl or baking pan. Be sure the curd is not deeper than 2 inches. Press a piece of plastic wrap against the top of the curd, or glide some butter over the surface. This will prevent a layer of thickened curd or skin from forming on the top. Chill for 4 hours or overnight. The curd should be kept in refrigeration.

6. Prepare the tart crust in the blind baked fashion and cool. Fill the tart crust with the chilled curd and garnish with fresh berries.

chapter thirteen

COMFORT FOODS

MEATLOAF FOR COMPANY

Serves 6 to 8

3 slices white bread, crusts removed

1 large carrot, peeled and cut into ¼-inch thick rounds

2 ribs celery, cut into ½-inch pieces

1 medium yellow onion, peeled, chopped into large pieces

2 cloves garlic, peeled and minced

½ cup flat-leaf parsley, loosely packed

½ cup plus 3 tablespoons ketchup

2 teaspoons dry mustard, or 2 tablespoons Dijon or yellow prepared mustard

1 pound ground beef (or all ground turkey)

½ pound ground pork—not pork sausage (you can use all beef if you prefer)

2 large eggs, beaten

2 teaspoons salt

1 teaspoon freshly ground pepper

2–4 dashes hot pepper sauce (Tabasco), or to taste

Topping:

2 tablespoons brown sugar

1 tablespoon prepared mustard

2 teaspoons dried or 1 tablespoon fresh rosemary (chopped)

1. Preheat oven to 400°F.

2. Place bread in the bowl of a food processor. Process until fine crumbs. Transfer bread crumbs to a large mixing bowl.

3. Place the carrot, celery, onion, garlic, and parsley in the bowl of the food processor. Process (using pulses) until vegetables are finely minced. The mixture should be a fine mince, with some tiny pieces of carrot and vegetables still recognizable. Transfer vegetables to bowl with the bread crumbs.

4. Add ½ cup ketchup, 2 teaspoons mustard, eggs, salt, pepper, and hot sauce. Using your hands, lightly knead the ingredients until thoroughly combined. Be sure not to overwork the mixture. Mix just until combined.

5. Set a small wire baking rack into an 11x17 inch baking pan. Cut a an 8x11 inch piece of parchment paper and place over center of rack to prevent meatloaf from falling through. Using your hands, form an elongated loaf covering the parchment. It will be approximately 10 inches long, 5 inches wide, and 3 inches tall.

6. Place the remaining 3 tablespoons ketchup, remaining 2½ teaspoons mustard, and brown sugar in a bowl. Mix until smooth. Using a pastry brush or the back of a spoon, generously brush the glaze over loaf.

7. Bake 75 to 90 minutes or until thermometer inserted in center of loaf registers 160°F. Let meatloaf cool on rack 15 minutes. Slice into 1-inch thick slices.

FRUIT COBBLER

This cobbler has been a crowd pleaser at our house for years. I've been making it in the kitchen oven or in the wood-fired oven. Fresh or frozen fruits work well.

Makes 6 to 8 servings

½ cup butter

1 cup all-purpose flour

¾ cup granulated sugar

2 teaspoons baking powder

½ cup milk

4 cups fresh or frozen fruit (blueberries, raspberries, blackberries, peaches, or plums in any combination)

½ cup sugar

1. Preheat oven to 350°F.

2. Melt butter and pour into a baking dish. I prefer an oval ceramic dish if possible.

3. In a medium bowl, combine flour, ¾ cup sugar, and the remaining dry ingredients, and stir to blend.

4. Add the milk and stir to blend. Don't overmix, just stir to combine all the ingredients.

5. Using a large spoon, place spoonfuls of the batter on top of the butter. Don't stir or mix. Some of the butter will be peeking out between the spoonfuls of batter.

6. Depending on the sweetness of the fruit, toss it with ⅛ to ¼ cup sugar. Place the fruit over the dough—don't stir! You will have a layer of butter, then batter, then fruit on top.

7. Place in the oven and bake for 45 minutes. The dough will puff. Depending on the juiciness of the fruit, the cobbler may require a longer baking time. The dough should be golden and spring back. Be very careful when testing for doneness. The sugar and fruit juices are very hot.

8. Allow to cool for a few minutes, then serve with vanilla ice cream.

> **TIP!** If using frozen fruits, they can go on top of the batter without thawing. Fresh peaches and plums should be sliced into ½-inch slices.

Four Cheese and Chicken Enchiladas

One of my cooking classes included a group of friends who simply wanted to cook together. They loved spicy, Mexican food. This is one of the recipes we made. It's adapted from a recipe from by Bobby Flay.

4–6 servings

12 soft corn tortillas

For the Enchilada Sauce:

2 ancho chiles (dried)

3 tablespoons vegetable oil

1 large red onion, finely chopped

3 cloves garlic, finely chopped

1 tablespoon ground cumin

1 tablespoon dried oregano

1 cup dry white wine

1 (16 ounce) can plum tomatoes, pureed

2 cups homemade chicken or vegetable stock

Salt and freshly ground pepper

For the Sauce:

1. Bring 2 cups of water to a boil in a small saucepan. Add chiles, remove from heat, and let sit for 30 minutes.

2. After the chiles have softened, remove stems and seeds, place in food processor with ¼ cup of the soaking liquid, and pulse, pureeing until smooth.

3. Heat oil in a medium saucepan over medium-high heat. Cook onions until soft and translucent, about 5 minutes.

4. Add garlic and cook for 1 minute, being careful not to burn the garlic. Add cumin and oregano and cook to combine, about 1 to 2 minutes. Add ancho puree and cook for 2 to 3 minutes.

5. Add wine, tomatoes, and stock and cook for 20 to 25 minutes or until slightly thickened. Season with salt and pepper, to taste.

For the Four Cheese and Chicken Filling:

8 ounces soft goat cheese (chèvre)

3 cloves garlic, coarsely chopped

¼ cup freshly grated Romano, Asiago, or Parmesan cheese

1 cup grated Chihuahua cheese or Mexican cheese

1 cup grated white cheddar or medium cheddar cheese

2–3 boneless/skinless chicken breasts, cooked and shredded/chopped

2 tablespoons fresh lime juice

¼ cup finely chopped cilantro

Salt and freshly ground pepper

Place cheeses, garlic, lime juice in a bowl and mix until smooth. Season with salt and pepper, and fold in the cilantro, add the chicken.

To assemble:

1. Spread ½ cup of sauce on the bottom of a baking dish.

2. Dip tortillas in the sauce to coat both sides. Spoon about 2 tablespoons of the cheese and chicken filling on each tortilla. Roll to close and place seam side down in the baking dish. It may be a tight squeeze.

3. Pour 1½ cups sauce over the enchiladas and top with grated cheese.

4. Bake 20 to 30 minutes, or until the enchiladas are heated through and the cheese is melted and bubbling.

5. Remove from the oven and sprinkle with chopped cilantro and chopped green onions. Pass extra sauce and sour cream.

Winter Sunday Football Chili

In Wisconsin, Sunday football is a tradition. Nearly every Sunday during the season I make a pot of chili. It simmers as we cheer on our team.

Serves 6 to 8

1 pound ground beef

1 tablespoon olive oil

1 yellow onion

2–3 cloves garlic

2–3 tablespoons chili powder

2 teaspoons ancho chili powder

1/4–1/2 teaspoon cayenne pepper

2 dashes hot pepper sauce

4 tablespoons dried cumin

2 teaspoons salt

1 teaspoon ground black pepper

1 1/2 teaspoons dried oregano leaves

1 28-ounce can tomato puree

1 15-ounce can diced tomatoes or 2 tomatoes peeled and seeded

2 16-ounce cans dark red pinto beans

Garnishes:

Shredded cheddar cheese

Sour cream or Greek yogurt

Chopped onion or green onion

Corn chips

1. In a large enameled roasting pan or stock pot, brown the ground beef over medium heat. Drain well and set aside.

2. In the same pan, heat the oil and cook the onion until soft and translucent, about 5 minutes. Smash the garlic on the cutting board with a chef knife (keep blade away from hands), and then chop. This will help the skin of the garlic slip off easily.

3. Add the chopped garlic and cook for another 2 minutes.

4. Add the cooked ground beef back into the pan.

5. Add the chili powders, cumin, oregano, salt, and pepper. Stir to combine and cook for 1 to 2 minutes over medium heat.

6. Add the tomatoes, and puree. Add 1 cup water. Stir to combine. Heat to a boil, then reduce to a simmer. Simmer at least 1 hour or longer, partially covered. If chili reduces too much, add more water.

7. Fifteen minutes before you're ready to serve, open beans and rinse. Add to the chili, and stir to heat through. Adjust seasoning by adding more hot sauce, salt, and/or pepper. Ladle into bowls and serve with garnishes for topping.

GARY'S EGG SCRAMBLE

Gary was already cooking a lot when I met him. He took cooking classes and takes pride in his ability to wield the giant Asian cleaver. One of his specialties is eggs. He can poach an egg like nobody's business. He's also mastered an impromptu egg scramble. He's the king of chopping and fine chops much better than I can. This recipe allows for a lot substitutions and creativity. Make it spicy or tame. The trick is to keep the potato pieces small so they cook quickly and evenly.

4 large servings

6 large eggs, loosened

1 cup grated cheese (cheddar, pepper-jack, Swiss)

1/2 cup finely grated Parmesan, Asiago or Romano

2 medium potatoes, peeled and diced into 1/4–1/2 inch cubes

1 cup mushrooms, sliced and chopped

1 red or yellow onion, peeled and finely chopped

1 clove garlic, finely chopped

1/2–1 jalapeno pepper, seed removed, finely chopped

1/2 green pepper, seeds removed, finely chopped

2–3 ounces ham or turkey, cubed in 1/4–1/2 inch cubes (optional) or 3–4 ounces smoked salmon

1 tablespoon olive oil

1/2 teaspoon hot red pepper flakes

1/2 teaspoon salt

1/2 teaspoon pepper

1. In a large nonstick skillet or frying pan, heat the oil over medium heat. Add the potatoes, and saute until tender about 5 to 6 minutes. The potatoes will brown, but shouldn't burn.

2. Add the onion and green pepper. Continue to cook until vegetables soften, about 5 minutes.

3. Add the garlic and mushrooms, stir to heat through.

4. Add the ham and continue cooking to mix through. Add the red pepper flakes, salt, and pepper. When all the ingredients are cooked, switch to a heat-resistant spatula and stir in the eggs. Stir quickly to scramble.

5. As the eggs are finishing, fold in the cheeses. When the eggs are completely cooked through, divide between plates and serve with warm toast.

PASTA A LA CARLA

Gary and I took a cooking class in Tuscany. Our class assistants were two sisters who worked at the guest house estate as housekeepers. When classes are in session, they work as class assistants, prepping ingredients, setting up a beautiful buffet table setting, and lending a hand as we prepared delicious Tuscan meals. One day Carla guided us through her family's pasta sauce. No recipe. She presented only the ingredients and helped us prepare the best sauce I've ever tasted. She spoke only a few words of English, like "hi" and "okay." The rest she communicated with her twinkling eyes and busy hands. We could chop and chop our vegetables and ask, "okay?" She would shake her head no, and make chopping motions with her hands: more chopping. The vegetables are minced very fine so they melt away into the sauce. Pair with your favorite pasta.

4 ounces pancetta, diced into ¼–½ inch cubes

1 red onion, finely minced

3 cloves garlic, finely minced

1 cup parsley, finely minced

1 medium carrot, finely minced

1 teaspoon granulated sugar

2 stalks celery, finely minced

2 cans San Marzano or plum tomatoes, drained, juice reserved (pass tomatoes through food mill)

½ teaspoon hot pepper flakes

2 tablespoons olive oil

1½ teaspoon salt

1 teaspoon ground black pepper

Freshly grated Parmigiana-Reggiano or Grana Padano cheese

1–2 pounds pasta (Fettuccine or spaghetti work well. Start with 1 pound, add more as needed.)

1. In a large dutch oven or large skillet, heat the olive oil over medium heat.

2. Add the pancetta and cook until lightly crisped and golden brown. Add the onion, carrot, and celery. Stir to combine and cook until the vegetables are tender. Try not to let the onion brown, about 4 to 5 minutes.

3. Add the garlic and cook for 1 more minute. Add the tomatoes, sugar, parsley, pepper flakes, salt, and pepper.

4. Add 1 cup water and ½ cup reserved tomato juice. Bring to a boil, and then reduce the heat to low.

5. Partially cover and simmer 30 to 45 minutes, until the sauce has reduced by approximately one third and has thickened. Keep the sauce simmering at a gentle bubble.

6. Adjust seasonings with more hot pepper flakes, salt, or pepper. Reduce the heat and cover the sauce while you prepare the pasta.

7. Prepare your pasta in salted, boiling water. The water should taste salty. When the pasta is al dente (just a bit of firmness to the bite), drain, and return to the pan. Swirl the pasta in the hot pan to dry the pasta, making it more receptive to holding the sauce. Add ladlefuls of sauce to the pasta, stirring gently until mostly covered.

8. Pour pasta and sauce into a large serving bowl. Add more sauce to the top, and pass cheese to finish.

Spaghetti and Meatballs

I love meatballs. Meatball sandwiches or spaghetti and meatballs are two of my favorite meals. It can be tricky to find a really good meatball. They can be rock hard, tasteless, or too mushy. I started experimenting and think I've created a winner. In Wisconsin, where fresh herbs are tricky to find in the winter, I've created a recipe using dried herbs.

Serves 4 to 6
(Makes about 24 meatballs)

1 pound ground beef (90/10)

½ pound ground pork (not pork sausage)

1 teaspoon salt

1 teaspoon ground pepper

¾ cup finely grated Grana Padano or Parmesan cheese

2 eggs

½ onion, finely minced

2–3 tablespoons chopped Italian parsley

1–2 tablespoons olive oil, for browning meatballs

1. Place the ingredients (except the oil) into a large bowl. Gently mix together. Don't overmix or overwork. With a very light hand, shape into slightly larger than golf-ball sized balls.

2. In a large skillet, heat the olive oil over medium-high heat. Add the meatballs. Don't try to move the meatballs for a few minutes because the meat will stick to the pan and break up the meatballs. When you are able to roll or pick up the meatballs with tongs, continue to brown on all sides. Repeat until all the meatballs have been browned. The outside should be browned, but the inside does not need to be completely cooked through. Place the meatballs on a paper-towel lined plate, and set aside.

For the sauce:

2 tablespoons olive oil

1 onion, finely chopped

4 cloves garlic

2 28-ounce cans whole peeled tomatoes (drained with juice reserved) passed through a food mill or pulsed 4–5 times in a food processor

2 7-ounce cans/jars tomato paste

2 tablespoons dried basil leaves

1 tablespoon dried oregano

½–1 teaspoon dried thyme

1 teaspoon salt

1 teaspoon ground black pepper

½ teaspoon dried red pepper flakes

½ cup red wine

1 teaspoon brown sugar

1 teaspoon red wine vinegar

3 tablespoons fresh parsley, finely minced

Freshly grated Grana Padano cheese for passing

1. In a dutch oven or large pan, heat olive oil over medium-high heat.

2. Add onions and cook until they are translucent, about 5 minutes. Try not to let the onions brown.

The Little French Bakery Cookbook

3. Add the tomatoes, herbs, garlic, wine, and sugar. Stir to combine, then heat to a boil. Reduce the heat and simmer, uncovered, for 1 hour. Adjust seasonings. You may need to add a bit more salt if you've used Grana Padano cheese in your meatballs. It's less salty than Parmesan.

4. When the sauce is ready, gently place the meatballs in a single layer in the sauce. Reduce the heat so the sauce is at a very low simmer. Cook the sauce and meatballs for 30 to 40 minutes.

5. While the meatballs are simmering, bring the pasta water to a boil. Prepare the pasta. When the pasta is al dente (tender to the tooth), drain and return to the pan on the stove, but without any heat under the pan. Swirl in the pan to remove any excess water and to dry the pasta a bit. Add two to three large spoonfuls of sauce to the pasta and stir. Pour the pasta onto a large serving platter. Top with more sauce and meatballs. Or, serve individual bowls of pasta, topping each with three to four meatballs.

TIP! Grana Padano or Parmigiano-Reggiano? Grana Padano is made with partially skimmed milk. It has a softer flavor and tends to be less nutty and salty than Parmigiano. The Po River in Italy produces this wonderful cheese. Parmigiano is made from whole and skimmed milk and must be produced in the cities of Parma, Reggio Emilia, Modena, Bologna, and Mantua. Because Grana Padano is more widely produced, it tends to be less expensive. I like Grana Padano's texture and flavor.

CARAMEL SAUCE

Perfect for ice cream or a special dessert topping.

½ cup (90 grams) granulated sugar

¼ cup (60 grams) water

⅔ cup (150 grams) heavy cream

1 tablespoon butter

Fleur de sel flakes (optional)

Place cream in a small saucepan and heat to a simmer. In another pan, add the water then sprinkle the sugar on top. Place pan over medium heat. Without stirring, heat the sugar and water until the caramel is amber in color. Carefully pour the warm cream onto the caramel. Be very careful. The cream will sputter and steam. Stir gently to dissolve any caramel bits. Pass through a strainer, stir in the butter, and cool. For salted caramel treats, drizzle caramel then sprinkle with fleur de sel.

TIP! Caramel is delicious and beautiful. It can also be dangerous to make. If this is your first time making caramel, there are a few safety tips you should know. First, place a large skillet/fry pan filled one third to one half full of water. Set near the stove. If the caramel begins to cook too quickly or burn, set your caramel pan into the fry pan. The caramel will stop cooking and prevent burning the sugar. Second, sugar burns are very bad. If you accidentally get hot sugar on your fingers, quickly rub the sugar off with a towel. Resist sticking your fingers in your mouth—you'll burn your lips or mouth, too. When you pour cream onto the sugar, hold the handle and place the pan so it's shielding you and your hand from the spattering sugar. Be sure your pan has tall sides to handle the steaming sugar and cream. And finally, sugar will quickly go from light to dark caramel. Never leave cooking caramel unattended. The sugar will continue to caramelize even if you reduce the heat. Have the cream ready to "stop" the caramel when it's the desired color.

Cheese Fondue

I love cheese. If you're in the mood for a wonderful, warm, delicious fondue, this is it. Serve it with a crisp green salad and big cubes of French baguette and vegetables. The dry white wine gives this fondue a great flavor. The cheese varieties melt nicely, not too gooey or stringy.

Serves 4 to 6

4 teaspoons cornstarch

Juice of ½ lemon (1–2 tablespoons)

1¼ cups Champagne, or dry white wine

1 large shallot, finely chopped

2 cups (about 8 oz) coarsely grated Gruyère cheese

1⅓ cups (about 4 oz) coarsely grated Emmenthal cheese

½ cup diced rindless Brie or Camembert cheese (about 3 ounces)

Generous pinch of ground nutmeg

Pinch of ground white pepper

1 French-bread baguette, crust left on, bread cut into 1-inch *cubes*

Broccoli, cauliflower, green pepper (optional dipping choices) chopped in large pieces

1. Stir cornstarch and lemon juice in a small bowl until cornstarch dissolves; set aside.

2. Combine Champagne/wine and shallots in a fondue pot or heavy medium saucepan (off the heat). Bring to a simmer over medium heat. Be very careful when cooking with wine as it can ignite.

3. Remove pot from heat. Add all cheeses and stir to combine. Allow the cheeses to melt slowly, stirring often.

4. Stir in cornstarch mixture.

5. Return fondue pot to low/medium heat and stir until cheeses are combined, smooth. The fondue will thicken and bubble. The thickening will take about 10 minutes. Season fondue with nutmeg and white pepper.

6. Keep warm in your fondue pot, or over very low heat. Using skewers, dip chunks of bread and chopped vegetable. If fondue thickens too much, thin with a few teaspoons of wine or Champagne, stirring to combine over heat.

Dad's Thanksgiving Dressing

Almost every family I know has their own version of Thanksgiving dressing. Whether it's made from scratch or out of a box, it's the one they think of when they think of the holiday meal. Our family is no exception. My grandma and my dad have always made this dressing. It was always cooked separately from the turkey. It's almost like a sausage bread pudding. We love it, and I hope you will too.

Serves 8 to 12 as side dish

1 large loaf white bread, sliced and crusts removed

1 large onion, chopped

1 1-pound tube ground sausage (something like Jimmy Dean)

2 tablespoons poultry seasoning

6 tablespoons butter

2 teaspoons ground black pepper

1 egg, loosened

1 teaspoon salt

1. Preheat oven to 350°F.
2. Tear the bread into 1–2 inch pieces, and set aside.
3. In a large skillet/frying pan; brown the sausage, drain, and set aside.
4. Wipe out the pan, then melt the butter. Add the onion and cook over medium heat until it is soft and translucent.
5. In a large mixing bowl, place the bread in the bowl and drizzle with water. The bread should be very damp, almost squishy. My dad used to hold the bread loaf under the faucet and run the water over the bread, then tear.
6. Add the egg, butter, onion, sausage, poultry seasoning, salt, and pepper. Stir together. Place the mixture in a large, buttered casserole dish. Bake uncovered for 45 to 60 minutes until golden brown and slightly puffed.

My Thanksgiving Dressing

My dad's dressing is great. That said, I needed to put my own spin on it and make it just a little different. The base recipe is the same, but I've added some additional goodies.

Serves 8 to 12 as side dish

1 large loaf white bread, sliced and crusts removed

3 cups chicken stock

1 large onion, chopped

1 1-pound tube ground sausage (something like Jimmy Dean)

2 tablespoons poultry seasoning

6 tablespoons butter

2 teaspoons ground black pepper

1 egg, lightly beaten

1 teaspoon salt

1 cup chopped pistachio nuts, almonds, or pecans (in any combination)

1 cup dried cranberries or dried cherries

The Little French Bakery Cookbook

1. Preheat oven to 350°F.

2. Tear the bread into 1–2 inch pieces, and set aside.

3. In a large skillet/frying pan, brown the sausage, drain, and set aside.

4. Wipe out the pan, and then melt the butter. Add the onion and cook over medium heat until it is soft and translucent.

5. In a large mixing bowl, place the bread in the bowl and drizzle with the chicken stock. The bread should be very damp, almost squishy. If the bread is still dry, you can add more stock or some water.

6. Add the egg, butter, onion, sausage, poultry seasoning, salt, and pepper. Stir together. Mix in the nuts and dried fruit.

7. Place the mixture in a large, buttered casserole dish. Bake uncovered for 45 to 60 minutes until golden brown and slightly puffed.

ROAST CHICKEN

Over the years, I've had several college-aged employees. At the end of the summer they go off to school, and I've got an empty nest. At one of our end-of-summer dinners, we were in a French restaurant bidding farewell. We started discussing things they'd be making in their dorms and apartments while away at school. I asked if they knew how to roast a chicken. Chicken, they asked? I told them they needed to know how to roast a chicken. They could roast it one day, have a meal, then have great sandwich and soup leftovers for a few days. My version combines the tips I've learned over the years.

1 4–5 pound roasting chicken	1 tablespoon olive oil
2 large yellow onions	1 tablespoon butter
1 smaller yellow onion	Salt
1–2 cloves garlic	Pepper
1 lemon	1 spring fresh rosemary

1. Preheat oven to 425°F.
2. Pat the chicken dry with paper towels.
3. Slice the top and bottom off the onions, then slice into three equal pieces, about ½–1 inch thick. Set aside.
4. Sprinkle the inside of the chicken with salt and pepper.
5. Using your fingertips, smear the butter on your hands then slide your fingers between the skin and the breast meat. Smear the butter under the skin.
6. Coarsely chop the rosemary and slide it under the skin, being careful not to puncture through the skin with the stem of the rosemary.
7. Place the large onion slices on the bottom of a roasting pan. The onions will serve as a rack for your chicken. Set the chicken on top of the onions.
8. Slice the small onion and lemon into quarters and insert into the cavity of the chicken. Smash the garlic and place inside the cavity. Pull the legs together, crossing slightly, and tie loosely together with cotton kitchen string. If you don't have any string, it's fine to skip this step. The string helps to hold the contents inside the chicken and helps roast the chicken more evenly.
9. Rub the outside of the chicken with olive oil, and then sprinkle with salt and pepper.
10. Place the roasting pan in the center of the oven. Bake for 15 minutes, then turn the oven to 375°F without opening the oven door. Bake another 50 minutes or until a thermometer inserted in the thigh registers 165°F.
11. Remove the pan from the oven. Cover the chicken with foil, and allow it to rest 10 to 15 minutes. Transfer to a serving platter, carve, and serve.

ACKNOWLEDGMENTS

There are so many people who helped make this book a reality.

Thank you to my family and friends near and far for listening, tasting, reading and helping test recipes. Special thanks to Caitlin, Diane, Kim, Larry and Maggie, Rita, Sara, Sharon and Stella for your extra special help in my kitchen and yours. Thank you Marge for just being you.

I have a wonderful team at The Little French Bakery. Jess, Jane, Keli and Phoebe have gone above and beyond to allow me the time to write, photograph and blog.

Amy Sullivan designed the cover, and continues to delight with her illustrations and design.

The photographs of me were taken by Michael and Heather Krakora of Krakora Studios. It was a fun day. Thank you. Lindsey, thank you for the great photo from our time in Ireland. A big thanks to the staff at the Camera Company for impromptu equipment help, service and technique tips.

A big thank you to my team at Skyhorse Publishing. My editor, Kristin Kulsavage, made a daunting process understandable to a first-timer.

I'd like to thank my family. Gary, you're the best husband in the world.

There are so many great chefs and food photographers before me who have paved the way. Thank you for all you have taught me. I am humbled by your talent.

METRIC AND IMPERIAL CONVERSIONS

(These conversions are rounded for convenience)

Ingredient	Cups/Tablespoons/ Teaspoons	Ounces	Grams/Milliliters
Almond flour	1 cup	3.4	101
Almond paste	1 cup	9.1	274
Almonds	1/2 cup	1.5	45
Baking powder	1 teaspoon	0.1	4
Baking soda	1 teaspoon	0.2	5
Bananas (mashed)	1 cup	8	240
Bread flour	1 cup	4.3	128
Butter	1/2 cup or 1 stick	4	120
Butter	1 cup=16 table-spoons= 2 sticks	8	230
Cake flour	1 cup	4	120
Cheese, shredded	1 cup	4	110
Chocolate chips	1 cup	6	180
Chocolate, chopped	1 cup	6	180
Cocoa, unsweetened	1/4 cup	0.8	23
Coffee, Instant-dry	1/4 cup	0.5	14
Cornstarch	1/4 cup	1	30
Cornstarch	1 tablespoon	0.3	8
Cream cheese	1 tablespoon	0.5	14.5
Egg white	1 large	1.3	38
Egg yolk	1 large	0.5	15
Flour, all-purpose	1 cup/1 tablespoon	4.5/0.3	125/8
Flour, whole wheat	1 cup	4	120
Fruit, dried	1 cup	4	120
Fruits or veggies, chopped	1 cup	5 to 7	145 to 200
Fruits or veggies, pureed	1 cup	8.5	245
Gluten free AP flour	1 cup	5.5	165

(Continued)

The Little French Bakery Cookbook

Ingredient	Cups/Tablespoons/Teaspoons	Ounces	Grams/Milliliters
Honey, maple syrup, or corn syrup	1 tablespoon	.75	20
Italian 00	1 cup	3.8	113
Liquids: cream, milk, water, or juice	1 cup	8 ounces	240 ml
Milk (1%)	1 cup	8	240
Molasses	1/4 cup	3	90
Oats	1 cup	5.5	150
Oats (quick cooking)	1 cup	3.1	94
Oats (traditional)	1 cup	3.5	105
Peanut butter	1/2 cup	4.8	143
Powdered milk	1/2 cup	4.3	129
Salt	1 teaspoon	0.2	5
Salt	1 teaspoon	0.2	6
Shortening, vegetable	1/2 cup	3.3	98
Spices: cinnamon, cloves, ginger, or nutmeg (ground)	1 teaspoon	0.2	5 ml
Sugar, brown	1 cup, packed	7.5	225
Sugar, brown, firmly packed	1 cup	7	200
Sugar, confectioners'	2 cups	8	240
Sugar, granulated	1 cup	7	210
Sugar, white	1 cup/1 tablespoon	7/0.5	200/12.5
Unbleached AP flour	1 cup	4.3	128
Vanilla extract	1 teaspoon	0.2	4
Vegetable oil	1/2 cup	3.7	111
Water	1 cup	4	120
Whole wheat flour	1 cup	4	120
Yeast, active dry	1 tablespoon	0.3	10

OVEN TEMPERATURES

Fahrenheit	Celsius	Gas Mark
225°	110°	¼
250°	120°	½
275°	140°	1
300°	150°	2
325°	160°	3
350°	180°	4
375°	190°	5
400°	200°	6
425°	220°	7
450°	230°	8

The Little French Bakery Cookbook

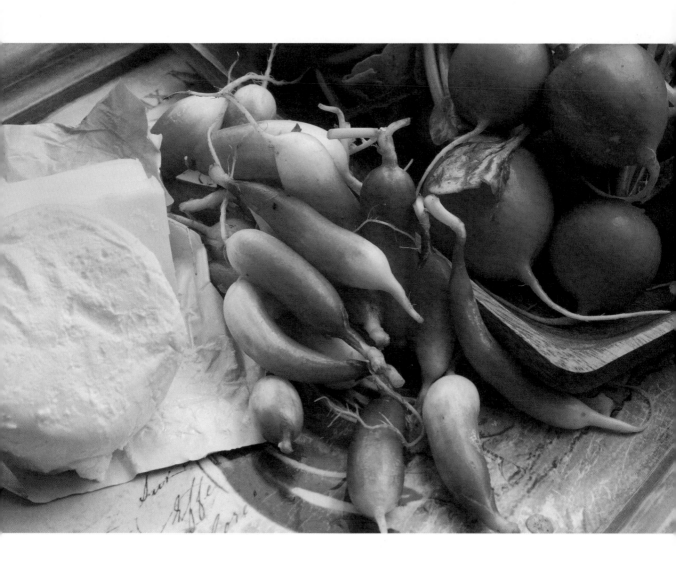

RECIPE INDEX